KU-054-965

Contents

Acknowledgement

I wish to thank Bob Coles, teacher, colleague, partner, friend and typist, for multifarious help at the various stages in the preparation of this manuscript. Some of it is based upon the structure and ideas of a course taught jointly at the University of York. This course exists no more, but we have both enjoyed and benefited from revisiting its content.

AP 19856.   HM 66 MAY

301.01 MAY

SOCIOLOGY SERIES
General Editor: Murray Morison

Sociological Theory

Mary Maynard

Senior Lecturer in Sociology,
Co-ordinator, Centre of Women's Studies,
University of York

LONGMAN
London and New York

LONGMAN GROUP UK LIMITED
Longman House, Burnt Mill, Harlow, Essex CM20 2JE, UK
and Associated Companies throughout the World.

Published in the United States of America
by Longman Inc., New York.

© **Longman Group UK Limited 1989**
All rights reserved; no part of this publication
may be reproduced, stored in a retrieval system,
or transmitted in any form or by any means, electronic,
mechanical, photocopying, recording, or otherwise,
without the prior written permission of the Publishers.

First published 1989
Second impression 1990
ISBN 0 582 00427 6

Set in 10/11pt Bembo, Linotron 202

Produced by Longman Singapore Publishers (Pte) Ltd.
Printed in Singapore

British Library Cataloguing in Publication Data

Maynard, Mary
  Sociological theory. – (Sociology in focus)
  1. Sociology. Theories
  I. Title II. Series
  301'.01

  ISBN 0–582–00427–6

Library of Congress Cataloging-in-Publication Data
Maynard, Mary, 1950–
    Sociological theory/Mary Maynard.
      p. cm. – (Sociology in focus series)
    Summary: Surveys the topic of sociological theory, examining both
  general theory and specific trends such as positivism and Marxism.
    Bibliography: p.
    Includes index.
    ISBN 0–582–00427–6
    1. Sociology. [1. Sociology.] I. Title. II. Series.
  HM66.M39 1989
301 – dc19   88–13543
                                                                  CIP
                                                                  AC

Series introduction

Sociology in Focus aims to provide an up-to-date, coherent coverage of the main topics that arise on an introductory course in sociology. While the intention is to do justice to the intricacy and complexity of current issues in sociology, the style of writing has deliberately been kept simple. This is to ensure that the student coming to these ideas for the first time need not become lost in what can appear initially as jargon.

Each book in the series is designed to show something of the purpose of sociology and the craft of the sociologist. Throughout the different topic areas the interplay of theory, methodology and social policy have been highlighted, so that rather than sociology appearing as an unwieldy collection of facts, the student will be able to grasp something of the process whereby sociological understanding is developed. The format of the books is broadly the same throughout. Part 1 provides an overview of the topic as a whole. In Part 2 the relevant research is set in the context of the theoretical, methodological and policy issues. The student is encouraged to make his or her own assessment of the various arguments, drawing on the statistical and reference material provided both here and at the end of the book. The final part of the book contains both statistical material and a number of 'Readings'. Questions have been provided in this section to direct students to analyse the materials presented in terms of both theoretical assumptions and methodological approaches. It is intended that this format should enable students to exercise their own sociological imaginations rather than to see sociology as a collection of universally accepted facts, which just have to be learned.

While each book in the series is complete within itself, the similarity of format ensures that the series as a whole provides an integrated and balanced introduction to sociology. It is intended that the text can be used both for individual and classroom study while the inclusion of the varied statistical and documentary materials lend themselves to both the preparation of essays and brief seminars.

PART 1

Introduction and overview

1   Theories and theorising

AMY, FIFTH FORMER: All the teachers are the same, they say 'Oh you should get this, you should pass in this', but they're no good to you when you're leavin'. I don't see the point in having 'em . . . [qualifications] people these days have got qualifications but they still haven't got jobs.
(P. Brown, 'Schooling for Inequality?' in *Education, Unemployment and Labour Markets*, edited by P. Brown and D. N. Ashton, Falmer Press, 1987)

ANGIE, FULL–TIME MOTHER: I think, well, I've spent all me youth tied in. Before you know you're going to be fifty and your life's done with, and you still haven't done nothing. In fact, one of the girls said to me, she was watching me cleaning up and she says: 'Isn't it funny, Mum, why people spend all their life doing things nobody notices? . . . look at you doing that dusting, nobody notices you know. . . . Nobody would notice if you never did it.' And I thought, 'Gee, thanks, I spend week in, week out doing things that nobody notices'. . . . Women seem to do jobs that nobody notices.
(Sue Sharp, *Double Identity*, Penguin, 1984)

It may seem strange to begin a book on sociological theory with two quotations from people who are not professional sociologists. But they provide us with some clues as to what theorising is about. In the first, Amy is replying to a question about job opportunities and making an effort at school. She is taking part in a study of comprehensive schooling. Amy is beginning to develop her own ideas about the usefulness of educational qualifications and is comparing them with the views held by others, especially teachers. She has her own theory. In the second quotation, Angie is discussing her experiences as a housewife with an interviewer researching women's domestic role. She is making the connection between her own household routine and the kind of invisible tasks performed by women in general. She has a theory about women's domestic work. Both Amy and Angie are thinking about their own particular circumstances and comparing them to those of others. They are trying to explore and understand, more fully, the situations in which they find themselves. This involves standing back from the routines of daily life and reflecting on ideas about them. In doing this both Amy and Angie are engaged in thinking theoretically.

We are all involved, on a day-to-day basis, in making theoretical sense of our lives and problems. Sometimes our ideas are quite straightforward. On other occasions they may be more complex. We may be concerned with unemployment and how it affects family life. We may be worried about falling out with our parents, experiencing sexism and racism, or why a teacher continually seems to pick on us. Whatever the issue at hand, our attempts to get to grips with our experiences of the world turn us into rudimentary social theorists. For, however unwittingly or unintentionally, we are seeking to *explain* the social world and those things about it which particularly affect us.

Differences between sociological and common-sense theory

In many respects the aims and purpose of sociological theory are similar to those of common-sense theory, described above. Particularly important are in-depth understanding and analysis of various aspects of the social world, together with *explanations* of how they were brought about and are likely to change. But there are also significant differences between sociological theory and our everyday attempts.

Firstly, sociology is able to take a more informed and far-seeing view of the world. This is because it draws on information and material which may have little connection or relevance to us personally. There are things that affect our lives, for example, which we may not know about, either because they are not

immediately observable or because we have not directly experienced them ourselves. We cannot actually *see* the education system
failing working–class pupils and reproducing social disadvantage,
although evidence collected from educational reports and statistics
may provide good grounds for believing this to be the case. The
fact that I am white and am not therefore subjected to racist
prejudice and discrimination should not lead me to conclude
that racism does not exist. Similarly, men may have to accept that
women are oppressed, even though they cannot experience
that oppression themselves and may not regard themselves
personally as oppressors. Each of us inhabits only a tiny part
of a complex and culturally varied world. It would be foolish to
imagine that the details and subtleties of this can be understood
on the basis of individual experience alone.

One implication of this argument is that we may have to come
to terms with viewing the world in ways which are the opposite
of those commonly held to be 'true'. It is widely believed, by
teachers and parents alike, that employers pay particular attention
to school qualifications in selecting school leavers for jobs.
Sociological research, however, points to a different and more
complex process: that in job interviewing employers take note of
such factors as appearance, character and work experience and
relatively little notice of examination performance. Indeed,
employers only seem to regard examination results as indirectly
indicating other qualities they are looking for. Sociology may
well, then, challenge and contradict our common–sense assumptions about the world and how it operates.

A second way in which sociological theory differs from
everyday theory is that it attempts to be much more systematic.
In ordinary life our ideas are sometimes based upon misunderstanding, ignorance and even prejudice. Further, it is quite possible for individuals simultaneously to hold views which are both
conflicting and contradictory. In sociological theory *clarity, consistency and coherence* are the aim, although they are not necessarily
easy to achieve. This means that the elements which make up a
theory should be clearly expressed. They should follow on from
each other and not contradict each other, and the relationship
between them should be explicitly stated. As Anderson *et al.*
explain it, 'What this means is that arguments have to be spelt out
to an extent unusual in everyday life; laying out all the steps as
clearly as possible. It is a requirement which leaves everything

open to critical inspection.' (Anderson, Hughes and Sharrock, *The Sociology Game*, Longman, 1985, p. 20)

A third difference between sociological and everyday theory is that sociological thought gives rise to *philosophical* problems, which do not necessarily occur in our everyday theorising. Such problems are related to the reflexive and self-conscious way in which sociologists go about theorising. They involve such questions as: what *sort* of knowledge have I got? is sociology a science and, if so, what kind of science is it? what do we mean by 'explanation' and when is an explanation adequate? and should sociology focus on society and patterns of human relationships or on individuals? The point to notice here is that sociological theorists disagree about the answers to such questions. They argue about the status of their theories and about the assumptions behind them. Some of these differing points of view will be discussed in subsequent chapters of this book.

What is sociological theory?

At its most simple, sociological theory involves exploring the *relationships* between different areas and kinds of social life. It is concerned with the conditions under which certain processes and patterns of structure or conflict are likely to occur. It involves *classifying* aspects of the social world, providing an *understanding* of them and looking for the *causes* of and *explanations* for them. This definition of theory has necessarily to be abstract because different theories seek to examine the social world at different levels of analysis. Some sociologists explore the broad pattern of social organisation which underpins the socio-economic system known as 'capitalism'. Others focus on particular sub-areas of society (institutions) such as education, the family or the occupation structure. Yet others examine more individualistic concerns, such as the impact of 'naming' (labelling) in the development of a 'career' of deviance or crime – for example, that of a football hooligan. In each of these instances theory will be used to probe deeply into the nature of society with the aim of uncovering how it works. But the *level* at which the theory is pitched is different.

Concepts

Theories are built from 'concepts'. As users of language, we all employ concepts. Words, the language of concepts, allow us to organise and relate our perceptions of the world together by classifying phenomena into general categories. Concepts isolate particular features of the world. They strive to communicate a uniform meaning about these features to all those who use them. Concepts are, therefore, short–hand ways of talking about aspects of the world, which do away with the necessity of having to describe every detail about them. The concepts of 'dog' and 'cat', for instance, enable us to distinguish different types of four-legged animals in the everyday world. In the natural sciences, concepts such as 'atom' or 'neutron' draw attention to particular properties of the physical world. In sociology, concepts such as 'anomie', 'youth subculture' or 'the ideology of domesticity' point to aspects of social life which are considered worthy of investigation and analysis.

The concepts used in sociology have three further characteristics which should be mentioned. Firstly, they are used at all levels of analysis. This means that they are employed when focusing on individuals or groups (as with the idea of 'deviant career'); or when analysing the general characteristics of a whole society (as in 'capitalism').

Secondly, concepts give us particular ways of looking at the world and of trying to understand it. They unite sets of ideas together. The concept 'capitalism' thus conjures up a picture of a society based upon private capital and wealth, the profit motive and class divisions. How we perceive and evaluate the world is, therefore, influenced by the concepts we use. They help to shape the sorts of questions we may ask about it and the kinds of answers which are likely to be obtained.

Thirdly, although an individual theorist may take great pains to define precisely what she or he means by particular concepts, difficulties and confusion can arise when there are differences of opinion or emphasis. A good example of this can be seen in the concept of 'class', where many definitions may be found, from those based on occupation alone to those stressing the relationship of the type of work done in a job to ownership of industrial resources. It is sometimes not easy to reach a clear consensus about the precise meaning of every sociological concept. For this reason, attention needs to be paid to how a particular concept is being defined, within the context of a specific theory.

Personal experience and beyond

It has already been suggested that sociological theorising means couching our analysis in terms of systematic arguments and ideas of which we ourselves do not necessarily have any direct experience. It is this which enables sociologists to talk about aspects of social life which may not be part of their own life history. It should not be thought, however, that personal experience has no relevance at all to theory. Much of the recent feminist literature, for example, has been important in indicating the significance of taking seriously what particular groups, in this case women, have to say about their lives. Women's accounts of sexual harassment and rape, for instance, have led to the extension and development of our more theoretical understanding of gender inequality. Nevertheless, it must be emphasised that most sociological theory involves going beyond immediate experience. This is because most things which interest sociologists can only be explained by looking, in part, at factors and relationships which exist outside our immediate circumstances and control.

Theory, policy and social change

Sociological theory is important because it gives us a deeper understanding of what is going on around us. It is also essential if we have any interest in promoting social change. This is because programmes of action can only be meaningful if they are rooted in a full analysis of current circumstances and how they have been brought about. To put it bluntly, it is impossible to devise a programme of change without some idea of which issues are central and how they might be confronted. It is the intention of some sociologists that their theory be directed to this purpose.

Sociological theory is also significant because 'empirical facts', such as those about suicide or unemployment, are always mediated through the language of theory. This means that 'facts' do not speak for themselves, but are socially constructed in the ways that they are put together and interpreted. This aspect of the social world will be discussed in a later chapter. For now it is sufficient to note that to understand 'facts' and the empirical side of sociology, we also need to understand the theoretical language and concepts which are being used to describe them. For, as we have already seen, concepts are very influential in determining how we perceive the world.

Sociological theory: types, disagreements and debates

Sociological theory is a highly varied activity, with different concerns, focuses and emphases. There are those theories which attempt to map out the subject matter of the discipline. These are concerned with the nature of the social world and the kinds of processes and mechanisms through which it operates. They are concerned with *ontology*. The theoretical work of Talcott Parsons and some of Marx's analysis of capitalism are examples of this sort of approach.

Another kind of theory is, paradoxically, concerned with method and with how the social world could or should be studied. These are theories about *epistemology*. Durkheim's *The Rules of Sociological Method*, and the various types of ethnomethodology, would be examples here. A different sort of theory has a *substantive* focus. Here the emphasis is either on the relationship between particular aspects of the social world – for example, class and education, or gender and leisure – or understanding in some detail the processes going on in specific areas of social life. Recent work on unemployment and changes in the labour market in the 1980s would be an example of this.

Within each of these broad types of theory, however, there are several divisive issues. Some theorists, for instance, want to produce theories which look like those of the natural sciences. Others believe that sociology is a different kind of science from natural science and therefore needs to be conducted and written in a different kind of way. There are also those who argue that sociology is not a science and should not pretend to be one.

There is disagreement too over the extent to which sociology should be ethically committed or value-neutral. Should theory be explicitly used in the service of ethical, moral and political issues or disassociate itself from judgements which are clearly value-laden? This dispute has been with sociology for a long time. Weber, for example, believed in value-neutrality and was very critical of those who used their academic work for political purposes. Marx, on the other hand, developed his theories as part of a political movement to overthrow the capitalist system. His thinking is, therefore, intentionally political and revolutionary.

Given these various orientations, it is scarcely surprising that a bewildering assortment of theories (functionalism, symbolic interactionism, phenomenology, ethnomethodology, structuralism and so on) has emerged. How can we make sense of this theoretical jungle, which Anthony Giddens has likened to a 'veritable Babel'?

Classifying sociological theory

Sociological theory has never comprised a single, unified body of thought accepted by everyone in the discipline. The nearest there has ever been to a dominant theory in sociology was during the post-war period, up until the late 1960s, with the structural functionalism of Talcott Parsons. But it never stood completely on its own. As Ian Craib has pointed out, in the USA there was always the alternative, if less popular approach, generally called 'symbolic interactionism'. In Britain, the main opposition came from what became known as the 'conflict approach', based mainly on the work of Max Weber. There was also some interest in Marxist thought, although little of this permeated the work of sociologists.

The political struggles of the 1960s led to some dramatic changes in sociological theory to the extent that there is now little work continuing in the strict structural-functional tradition. The Vietnam War, the Civil Rights movement in America, the development of the 'second-wave' women's movement – all gave rise to the criticism that the Parsonian model of consensus, harmony and equilibrium was unable to analyse or account for a society in upheaval and conflict. Alternative approaches, which had previously been ignored, took on a new vitality. Phenomenology was 'rediscovered', symbolic interactionism became respectable, ethnomethodology was created and Marxism discussed with a new vigour. The disintegration of the dominance of Parsonianism led to what Giddens has referred to as a 'squabbling diversity of schools of social theory'. Amid such confusion it became important for sociologists to find a way of categorising the emerging types of theory. This was necessary so that they could sort out the similarities and differences between them, judge which were the most significant and begin to evaluate the newly available approaches.

Initially these attempts tended to suggest dichotomies, that the whole of sociological theory could be divided into two categories only. Thomas Wilson, for example, distinguished 'normative' from 'interpretive' sociology. Alan Dawe contrasted theories which focused on the 'problem of order' from those focused on the 'problem of control'. David Walsh suggested that the choice was between 'positivistic' and 'phenomenological' approaches. Broadly speaking, 'normative', 'problem of order' and 'positivistic' theory were seen as concentrating on the social system, stressing the need for consensus in society and emphasising how individuals were constrained, through socialisation and the learning of societal values. 'Interpretive', 'problem of control' and 'phenomenological' theory, by contrast, were regarded as focusing on individual actors, the interaction between them, and their ability to control the outcomes of their lives. In the first kind of theory the individual is seen as being constrained and moulded by society. In the second the emphasis is upon the possibility of individuals actively constructing different meanings about, and understandings of, their social situation and thus retaining control, if not actively bringing about social change.

Subsequently sociologists have tried to develop more sophisticated ways of classifying theory than these simple dichotomies. A widely accepted way of doing this is to present sociology as a set of *perspectives*. A perspective is usually regarded as a collection of theories, with ideas and methods which constitute a more or less unified approach to the conceptualisation of sociology's subject matter. A perspective, it is argued, allows us to discuss together sociologists with similar ideas, theories, methods and arguments. Sociology is often presented as having three such perspectives: functionalism, interpretivism and materialism. These are further described in chapters 2, 3, 4, and 5.

What is wrong with using 'perspectives'?

As a simplifying device directing us to certain sociological debates and helping us to make sense of what is going on theoretically, perspectives may be a useful way of organising sociological theory.

They also, in the form in which they are usually constructed, sensitise us to the origins of sociology in the diverse positivist, interpretivist and materialist traditions. Each can be seen to have strong roots in nineteenth-century philosophical debates. Yet, increasingly, sociologists are raising problems about classifying theory in terms of perspectives. Five major criticisms can be made.

Firstly, there is no real agreement as to how many perspectives there are and what they are to be called. Functionalism, interpretivism and Marxism may be the most common, but other categories and labels are also to be found. O'Donnell, for example, distinguishes only between structural and interpretive perspectives and then refers to subdivisions within these. Collins identifies what he calls the conflict, Durkheimian and microinteractionist traditions. Cuff and Payne focus on structuralism, with its consensus and conflict variants, symbolic interactionism and ethnomethodology as perspectives. Such differences cause confusion and may lead to misunderstanding.

Secondly, the perspectives approach implies that there is a unity of intention and direction between those writers placed in each category. It will be argued in chapters 2–5 that this is by no means the case. Theorists are frequently put together under the same label when, in fact, there are more differences than similarities between them. The writings and intentions of Max Weber and the ethnomethodologist Harold Garfinkel are, for example, very different, although they are often put together in the same perspectives box. The work of the Frankfurt School and of Althusser have divergent emphases, although they are both labelled 'Marxist'. The perspectives approach tends to underplay these differences. It implies cohesiveness and ignores variations between theorists. There tend to be as many differences *within* particular perspectives as there are between them.

Thirdly, perspectives are presented as unchanging, but sociology is developing all the time. Further, adopting a perspectives approach means that there are only a limited number of categories in which a theorist can be placed. Yet there are many theorists who do not fit easily into *any* of the pre-defined boxes. These writers tend to be ignored in books and courses on theory which slavishly follow the perspectives approach. Examples of theorists who are usually overlooked, but who will be considered in this book because of their contribution to sociology, are Sigmund

Freud, Michel Foucault, Jurgen Habermas and Anthony Giddens, as well as a range of feminist authors.

Fourthly, it is often assumed that, within each perspective, there is a correspondence between the assumptions about the social world found in theory and those used in methods of research. This implies that each perspective has its own particular set of research techniques which are accepted by each sociologist whose work comes under its rubric. Thus functionalism is equated with positivism and interpretivism with strategies such as those of participant observation. But this forces a unity between theory and methods where one does not exist. As chapters 2 and 3 will make clear, functionalism and positivism are by no means identical or related. In Chapter 4, dealing with interpretivism, it will be pointed out that Weber certainly did not use participant observation nor Garfinkel ideal type analysis. There is, then no unambiguous fit between theory and methods. Rather, sociologists tend towards pragmatism in the research techniques which they adopt.

Finally, it can be argued that accepting perspectives makes the use of theory appear to be a rather sterile business. Sociology is depicted as the routine application of pre-given labels. It is made to seem as though the sociologist merely has to decide which perspective seems appropriate, and then apply it to the problem at hand. This portrays sociological perspectives as *competing* and makes it necessary to choose between them, thereby giving priority to one and only one. It also conveys an image of theory as comprising ideas which can be 'mugged up' and learnt parrot-fashion. But a more realistic view of how sociologists go about their work is to emphasise the processes of *theorising*, rather than the product, theory. Theorising is a creative and innovatory activity which is essential to any attempt at understanding the social world. Further, it is likely to involve drawing upon a range of approaches and ideas, rather than a set of views dictated by a particular perspective.

Sociological pragmatism

So far in this chapter we have explored the *general* nature and characteristics of sociological theory. The next chapters focus on the *specifics* of individual theories. It should be clear from the preceding section that this book is not written from a 'perspectives' standpoint, even though its format may suggest this to be the case. Rather, the intention behind the next four chapters is to look at the differences, as well as the similarities, between those who are often put into the same perspectival category. The aim is to challenge the notion that distinctive and separate perspectives exist. Instead, the rest of this book sets out to demonstrate that sociology is characterised by a range of theories, each of which necessitates consideration in its own right. I refer to such a stance as *sociological pragmatism*.

Sociological pragmatism has two main features. Firstly, it suggests that sociological theory is *pluralistic* rather than *linear* and *cumulative*. By this is meant that the intention behind theorising is not to build up to one united theory. Rather, because the social world is made up of different social phonomena, each requires different kinds of theoretical understanding and explanation. We need different theories to do different things. There can, therefore, be no single theory which is able to explain the workings of the whole of the social world.

Secondly, pragmatism means that sociology is involved in *compromise*. In choosing theories and methods, we are influenced by the kind of problems that we want to address. We select those that seem appropriate to the particular task at hand. Theory can only be of service if we can learn from it and use it; if it can be actively employed in *doing* sociology. On this basis it is not particularly helpful to refer to theories in terms of whether they are right or wrong or fit in with our own particular political thinking. Rather, the question is whether they are more or less useful in investigating the issues to which they are being directed. This seems a much more practical basis for evaluation. When they are engaged in the actual doing of sociology, sociologists often choose a combination of strategies which the perspectives approach would deem to be incompatible or to be drawn from opposing camps. For example, a number of Marxist researchers have recently started to use ethnographic methods. It is this 'borrowing' from what would be regarded as different perspectives to which I am referring in the idea of 'compromise'. In the 'real' world of research such compromises happen all the time. It is this that makes the business of sociology a developing intellectual task and the process of theorising a challenge and not a chore.

PART 2

Sociological theories

2 Positivism: the science of society

In the previous chapter it was argued that the use of a sociological perspectives approach can be misleading in helping us to understand different aspects of sociological theory. One area where this can be seen most clearly is in a discussion of positivism and functionalism. These two kinds of sociology tend to be portrayed as if they are a theoretical unity containing similar aims and assumptions. Yet the term 'functionalism' covers a range of authors, some of whom (Malinowski and Radcliffe-Brown, for example) spent a lifetime in bitter and personal antagonism about what was entailed in the functionalist approach. Likewise, the label 'positivist' has come to have a variety of meanings, some of which are in opposition to and contradictory of each other. Indeed, so confusing has the word become that it has been suggested that it should be erased from the vocabulary of any self-respecting sociologist. In an attempt to bring out the difficulties involved when referring to 'positivism' and 'functionalism', the next two chapters will trace some of the major debates which have occurred about their meaning.

Nineteenth-century positivism

Sociology became established as a major discipline during the nineteenth century. Many of its early proponents were concerned that it should benefit from advances in scientific methods that had been made in other subjects, such as biology. Many scholars believed that the rapid advancement in scientific knowledge had been made possible through the general acceptance and usage of a particular set of techniques. These were regarded as applicable to all subjects involving the study of both the natural and the social worlds. For sociology to match the achievements of the other sciences it seemed necessary for it to adopt this scientific method.

Several distinctive aspects of nineteenth-century scientific work thus became the key ingredients of sociological theorising. Firstly, there was a commitment to 'the scientific perspective, a unity of approach across all disciplines. Auguste Comte (1798–1857), usually regarded as the founding father of sociology, claimed that the new science of society had to share the same overall methodological logic as the other sciences.

A second significant aspect of nineteenth-century sociological theory was the use of the techniques of the natural sciences, particularly biology. Charles Darwin (1809–82), for instance, had shown how the laws of natural evolution could be discovered through the painstaking collection and classification of facts. The development of his theory of evolution was made possible by the careful and systematic observation of the masses of animal and plant specimens collected during his pioneering voyages of discovery. The bedrock of science was taken to be the existence of facts. Science itself proceeded via the collection and observation of facts, leading to the development of theories on the basis of, and with constant reference to, these facts.

Thirdly, and again following the Darwinian tradition, there was a concern among nineteenth-century thinkers with evolution and progress. It was believed that there was a single process, that of evolution, which could be identified in all aspects of the universe, both animate and inanimate. Evolutionists held that the general path of the evolutionary process was from simple to complex structures, with component parts developing increasingly specialised functions. This is called 'differentiation'. Evolution was not thought to be just about differentiation, though, but to involve integration as well. If equilibrium was to be maintained in the face of growing specialisation of functions, then a process of integration was also required, with increasing mutual interdependence of the structurally differentiated parts.

A fourth feature of nineteenth-century science and sociology was the attempt to formulate theories in terms of general laws. Comte, for example, argued that two kinds of general laws could be established. These were related to the two major kinds of study in sociology: 'statics' and 'dynamics'. 'Statics' were concerned with discovering *'laws of coexistence'*. These laws governed the relationship between different parts of society and therefore involved exploring the functions and interrelationships between various elements of a social system. 'Dynamics' were concerned with discovering *'laws of succession'*, which governed social change and which were to be found in the transformations which had occurred in the nature and function of social institutions.

In summary, then, we can see that the shape of nineteenth-century sociological theory was based on a particular view of the nature of science. The significant elements of this were: commitment to a unitary scientific perspective; the observation and classification of all known facts; acceptance of the evolutionary model; the establishment of universal laws. This approach was known as *positivism*.

It is important to emphasise that, at this stage in its development, positivism involved using an *inductive* approach to theorising. Induction refers to a method of approaching theories from supposedly pre-existing facts. It means building upwards in a knowledge hierarchy from facts, which are descriptive, to theories, which are explanatory.

Durkheim's positivism

Of the second generation of sociologists, perhaps the most important in the development of the positivist tradition was Emile Durkheim (1858–1917). Durkheim insisted even more strongly than Comte on the need for sociology to be regarded as an autonomous and distinct discipline. Like Comte he felt that recognition of such autonomy did not mean that the study of social phenomena should be carried out differently from how things were done in the natural sciences. For Durkheim, social facts had a moral dimension which was missing in the natural world, but they still had 'to be treated as things' in the same way as natural objects. Durkheim believed that every science, including sociology, advanced through making careful inductive generalisations based upon the observed regularities in social facts. Sociology should thus be seen as the natural science of society.

Durkheim's first attempt to produce a natural science of society is to be found in his book *The Division of Labour* (1893). The book focused on the classification of societies into two forms of moral and social order: mechanical and organic solidarity. Durkheim argues that, because moral facts are facts like any others, it is possible to observe them, describe them and develop laws which explain them. However, it is not easy to observe moral phenomena directly. If we wish to study them 'according to the method of the positive sciences', it is necessary to focus on *indirect* indices or expressions of their existence. Legal codes provide such an index of moral life because they are the formal expression of moral prescriptions. In the *Division of Labour* Durkheim examines the development of systems of law, claiming that this helps us to chart major changes in the moral order of society.

Durkheim was also concerned to clarify the nature of the subject matter of sociology. He attempted to specify the characteristics of sociology in such a way that it was clearly differentiated from other subjects, such as biology and psychology. Durkheim's attempt to define the social is to be found in his second book, *The Rules of Sociological Method* (1895) (see Reading 1).

The main thrust of Durkheim's argument is that no theory or analysis which begins from the 'individual' can successfully explain social phenomena. Not only is the subject matter of sociology the study of social facts, but these facts are external to individuals, and constrain them.

These points are linked to Durkheim's argument that if sociology is to be an autonomous discipline it must have an autonomous subject matter. Social phenomena must be treated as if they are real in themselves. They cannot simply be explained by looking at their constituent elements. In *The Rules of Sociological Method* he reiterated the views of many of his positivist predecessors in advocating: direct and objective observation of social facts; drawing up a description of facts after a study of many cases; classifying them into species; exploring the causes of variations between them through comparison; deriving any general laws which might have emerged in the course of earlier stages. These are the basic features of the *inductive* approach, and it was with these in mind that Durkheim then set out to produce his next work.

Durkheim's *Suicide* (1897) was particularly well suited to establishing his claim that sociology had its own particular subject matter. For suicide, on the face of it, appears to be the most private of acts which seems understandable only by looking at psychological facts. But Durkheim was not trying to explain why particular individuals commit suicide. Rather, he was seeking to understand the different suicide *rates* that were to be found in different types of societies and cultures.

Using a barrage of tables and statistics, Durkheim described different kinds of suicides and classified them into three main types. *Egoistic* suicide occurs when the ties bonding the individual to society are slackened or broken, leading to excessive individualism. *Altruistic* suicide, on the other hand, exists where the individual is too strongly integrated into society, so that the self has no independent value or autonomy. *Anomic* suicide occurs when people are left in a state of normlessness, as in periods of sudden and rapid economic change.

Durkheim then explored what caused different suicide rates. He explained that these were produced by differences in the patterns of social order in societies, and the degree to which social groups were integrated into them. When the degree of social cohesion in a society is either too loose or too strong, or when there is a lack of moral regulation and guidance in society, then suicides are more likely to occur. This led Durkheim to claim, in true positivist fashion, that he had established a general and universal law – that *suicide rates are inversely related to the degree of integration of the social groups of which the individual forms a part.*

Criticism of Durkheim's positivism

There have been many well-known criticisms of Durkheim's arguments in *Suicide*. For example, it has been pointed out that definitions of suicide vary from one country to another so that it is very difficult to compare suicide rates. Definitions of suicide may also change over time, both within and between societies. This failure to take account of the social processes through which official statistics, particularly suicide rates, are collected has been the subject of considerable analysis by Jack Douglas and Maxwell Atkinson. Douglas argues that, in every case of death, officials have to *interpret* the information that is made available to them (see Reading 2).

Although such points are important, they tend to be made by sociologists who are against positivism generally. They are hostile to Durkheim's work because they take it as an example of the positivist approach. But is it? Does Durkheim actually apply his own 'rules' in *Suicide*? At first sight *Suicide* is clearly inductive (proceeding to theory from the observation of social facts). Yet it is surely suspicious that Durkheim managed, supposedly through the 'scientific' study of suicide rates, to arrive at some of the major sociological concepts which he had been writing about throughout the previous decade. Durkheim seems to have decided *a priori* that concepts such as 'anomie', 'social solidarity' and 'collective conscience', which had had a significant place in his work prior to his study of suicide, would continue to be important. These concepts were derived from his abiding interest in the problem of social order and the ways in which it could be achieved.

A second issue is that positivism and Durkheim's own methodology suggested that 'facts' should be the bedrock of theory. But although, as we have seen, critics have accused him of treating suicide rates and statistics as unproblematic, Durkheim was far too intelligent and sophisticated to keep to that – even though his own 'rules' told him to do so. Durkheim showed that he was ingenious in his interpretation of facts, rather than naively letting them speak for themselves. For instance, in *Suicide* he argued that in Europe suicide was less likely to be found in Catholic than Protestant countries. This was due to the cohesiveness and moral direction provided by the Catholic Church. With England, however, Durkheim faced a problem, because the suicide rate there was lower than in other Protestant countries. To answer this point he argued that, under the Church of England, England had a parish system, and a higher proportion of clergy to laity than countries dominated by other types of Protestantism. This gave it some of the characteristics provided by the Catholic Church. In making such an argument, Durkheim was introducing his own ideas and views about England. He was offering his own specific and common-sense interpretation, rather than letting facts speak for themselves.

Rather than being a simple, slavish application of *rules*, then, *Suicide* draws on both pre-existing theories and knowledge. In doing this it also draws attention to some of the tensions and problems involved in nineteenth-century sociological positivism. Even then theorists found it difficult, if not impossible, to stick to the principles and methods which had been laid down. *Suicide* illustrates some of the ways in which proponents of positivism found themselves forgetting, or deliberately bending, the agreed rules.

Positivism in the twentieth century

We have seen that, in the nineteenth century, positivism took an *inductive* form. In this the distinctive hallmark of science was taken to be the collection and classification of facts from which theories and general laws subsequently emerged. During the first decades of the twentieth century, however, the emphasis on induction within positivism began to change. One of the problems with the inductive approach was that, although scientists could collect a mass of data and theorise about it, they had no way of telling whether further observations would produce information capable of completely disproving the theories they had generated. This is associated with the problem of *verification*. Consideration of this matter led to the introduction of ideas about 'testability'. Rather than collecting facts in an *ad hoc* fashion, it was suggested that tests should be devised in order to check the meaningfulness of theoretical statements.

One twentieth-century scholar to place great emphasis on the significance of testing was the philosopher Karl Popper. But Popper was also involved in another change of direction for positivism. This was the move from an *inductive* to a *deductive* emphasis. Deductivism involves the formulation of sets of hypotheses about the world in a way which makes testable statements deducible from them. On the basis of the test general laws and theories may be constructed. Now this formulation of positivism is a complete reversal of the nineteenth-century inductivist version. With deductivism, the idea of *testing* is crucial. For *inductivists*, it was how a theory was arrived at which was of critical importance. For *deductivists* it is having an independent and objective test.

Popper believes that scientific knowledge can never be absolutely 'proven'. He therefore claims that scientists should not waste time trying to prove that something is correct. Instead they must try and specify the conditions under which they would be willing to alter their interpretations of knowledge or reject a previously accepted theory.

Popper's view is that no scientific hypothesis can be regarded as established so long as the scientist knows only the evidence which confirms it and has not undertaken to discover evidence that disproves it. He therefore advocates 'falsification', the aim of which is to look for instances which are most likely to disprove the hypothesis which is being tested.

Contemporary positivism

Originally positivism meant an *inductive* approach to knowledge. From the 1930s it became identified with *deductive* analysis, which is the inverse of its original form. But in recent years sociologists have tended to confuse the debate over positivism. Firstly, they have implied that inductivism *and* deductivism entail the same kinds of approaches, which they do not. Secondly, they have made positivism into an all-encompassing stereotyped term which covers anything which smacks of science, objectivity, quantification and a belief in measurement. Yet few sociologists today actually embrace these aspects of positivism in a simplistic way even when they are practically involved in research activity which does involve quantification and hypothesis testing. Few believe that hypotheses can be easily and unproblematically formulated, that propositions can be clearly and unrefutably falsified, that measurement is simply a matter of technical precision, that the social world is no more complex to analyse than the physical world, and so on.

Instead, the sociological pragmatism discussed at the end of Chapter 1 is much more the order of the day. Most sociologists do not adhere to the idea that their work embodies complete value-neutrality. But neither do they advocate, or follow, its opposite – that sociology is mere subjectivism. They may not believe that 'facts' constitute the bedrock of social science, but many of us are prepared to conduct research '*as if*' social facts can be treated factually in order to proceed with substantive research work which we consider important. Sociologists are now largely dismissive of the idea of simply testing discrete hypotheses, but it is still necessary to have some idea of what one wants to research before embarking upon a study. In all these senses the stereotypical view of positivism is not only unsympathetic, but also unhelpful and misleading.

There is also another sense in which the debate over positivism has been misrepresented. Some sociologists have been criticised by others for using a supposedly positivist scientific model, although it should now be clear that the details of this are far more complex than is usually assumed. Yet the realistic and political fact is that it is often necessary to present sociology as 'scientific' in this way, in order to get funding for research. The main funding bodies for sociological research are still government departments and the research councils. Under their auspices money has been provided for studies of such diverse phenomena as unemployment, family relations, social effects of economic changes, poverty, inequalities of health and the operation of the welfare state. In order to engage in wide-ranging research of this kind, which is both socially and politically important, intellectual compromises become virtually inevitable. If sociologists wish to retain a voice within the public domain, if they wish to communicate with and influence public policy, then their studies have to appear to be rigorous, and the language used within their research reports responsive to those who control the 'purse strings'. The latter tend to have a particular image of what constitutes 'good' social science, and this approximates to what we have been discussing in this chapter under the heading of 'positivism'. In these circumstances, it is small wonder that researchers try to present their work in a 'scientific' (and hence 'positivistic') way, even though, in the day-to-day conduct of their work, they may deviate drastically from the 'pure' model. This is not a theoretical or philosophical argument *for* positivism, but it is one which attempts to explain why the apparent language of positivism is still so powerful.

3   Functionalist theory – and all that

At the same time as authors like Durkheim were establishing the methodological procedures for what they considered to be a properly *scientific* sociology, a genuinely distinctive theoretical perspective was also being developed. The origins of functionalism, as with positivism, were bound up with the advances made within biology in the nineteenth century. Here, as we have seen, the idea of social evolution was important, as was the use of biological analogies. Words such as 'function', 'structure' and 'equilibrium' were borrowed from biology to explain the 'anatomy and physiology of social life'.

Without doubt, Durkheim's works have been the most important influence on the development of functionalism in the present century. All of his work was coloured, to some degree, by a functionalist approach, and this can be seen most clearly in his book *The Elementary Forms of the Religious Life* (1915). Durkheim's focus of attention was Australian aboriginal culture and the mechanisms through which it was permeated with religious thought. He argued that, in such a culture, religious activity is functional because it facilitates the integration of different tribal groups. Although these groups lived separate and scattered lives in clans, religious ceremonies helped to show that they were in fact part of the same society, sharing the same social rules and values. An important aspect of this was worship of the 'totem'. The totem reminded individuals of their connection to the wider community and of the need to suppress their own specific needs and desires for the collective good. Such feelings were reinforced at religious ceremonies when, as a consequence of feasting and dancing, individuals experienced intense joy and strong emotions. Such a high degree of feeling was only possible in *collective* worship, when clan members felt overwhelming solidarity with those around them. Durkheim argued that religious worship helps to maintain the social order and promotes a moral unity within a tribal society. Religion, therefore, has the hidden significance or *function* of contributing to the existence of society by promoting social solidarity among its members.

The anthropological tradition of functionalism

Functionalism, as a well-articulated conceptual perspective, emerged in the twentieth century with the writings of two British anthropologists, Malinowski (1884–1942) and Radcliffe-Brown (1881–1955). Both of them were heavily influenced by Durkheim's work, as well as by their own studies of 'primitive' societies. Despite similarities in their intellectual backgrounds, however, there were a number of differences between them. Malinowski's approach was characterised by the assertion that every institution in society exists to fulfil particular human needs, such as food and shelter. In turn, the creation of certain patterns of social organisation and culture to fulfil individual needs gives rise to additional needs which must be met by further, and more elaborate, forms of social and cultural organisation. By such reasoning it is possible to identify three types of needs which shape society: the biological, the psychological and the cultural. Malinowski thus created the impression that social institutions arise in response to different types of need.

This line of argument is clearly both *teleological* and *tautological*; objections which, as we will see, are basic criticisms of the functionalist approach. It is teleological because it suggests that social phenomena have emerged in order to meet some '*purpose*', which they are then held to fulfil. But can *social* institutions spring up to fulfil 'purposes'? Such an explanation can be used to 'justify' any aspect of the social world in this *post hoc* fashion. The argument is also tautological (it uses circular reasoning). Here, cultural items are said to exist to meet a need of the cultural whole, while the cultural whole is supposed to exist to meet biological and psychological needs.

Whereas Malinowski started from an emphasis on individual needs, Radcliffe-Brown explained phenomena in terms of the social structure, especially its 'need' for solidarity and integration. For example, in analysing a lineage system, Radcliffe-Brown would first assume that some minimal degree of solidarity must exist in the system. Processes associated with lineage systems would then be assessed in terms of their consequences for maintaining this system. But this form of analysis also poses problems. While Radcliffe-Brown admits that the functional unity of a social system is a hypothesis and no more, he never says how such a hypothesis might be empirically tested, nor how much or how little functional unity would be necessary for a system to survive. Thus, what typically happens, with Radcliffe-Brown, as with other functionalists, is that it is assumed that a system *is* minimally integrated and surviving just because it exists and persists. But this also produces a *tautology*. It implies that if a system can be found, then it must have integrated parts because it *is* a system. Radcliffe-Brown frequently slips into just such a pattern of circular reasoning. In this he assumes that the fact of a system's existence *necessarily* requires that its existing parts, such as the lineage system, be viewed as contributing to its continuation. He can, therefore, only focus on the *positive* contribution made by a part of society to its existence but not on any possible negative or even neutral effects it may have.

There were numerous attempts to popularise functionalist theory between 1930 and 1960, and to apply the basic functionalist framework to advanced society. Kingsley Davis, in particular, was responsible for applying the functionalist framework to American society, and using it to explain such diverse phenomena as the stratification system and prostitution (see Reading 3). But many students recognised basic flaws in the functionalist framework. One writer who did much both to codify the weaknesses of the framework and to suggest remedies and revisions for it is Robert K. Merton.

Merton and the systematisation of functionalism

Merton's *Social Theory and Social Structure* (1949) anticipated and attempted to meet some of the criticisms of functionalism that became the focus of debate in the 1950s and 1960s. Merton claimed that functionalism needed to be substantially amended if it was to encompass the problems of complex, industrialised societies. His main concern was understanding the social consequences of particular institutions or items of culture – *item-centred functionalism*. Firstly, he argued that the term 'function' had to be precisely defined. It was necessary to separate the 'subjective' intentions of human actors from the concern of the sociologist with the outcomes of patterns of action. 'Social function', Merton says, refers to '*observable objective consequences*, and not to *subjective dispositions* (aims, motives, purposes)'. What a person intends to achieve may or may not coincide with the outcome of his or her action. It is the outcome *only* which is of interest to the functionalist and the sociologist. Merton separated the subjective and objective elements of functional analysis, by making a distinction between *manifest and latent functions*. Manifest functions are those social consequences which are intended and recognised by societal members. But social practices often have consequences which are neither intended nor recognised by those engaged in them. They have, in Merton's terms, latent functions.

Secondly, Merton was critical of the *postulates of 'functional unity'* and of '*functional universality*', which were widely incorporated within the functionalist approach. The first, which suggests that society is always integrated or in harmony, should be rejected, according to Merton. Instead of making societal integration a matter of *theoretical assumption*, Merton suggests that the degree of integration of a society must be treated as an *empirical question*. The second postulate, which indicates that every standardised social practice and cultural item has a function in society by virtue of its persistence, was also questioned. Merton suggested that a distinction should be made between an institution and its functions. To say that a society requires certain functions to be fulfilled is not the same as saying that any particular institution is therefore indispensable. The same functions may, in fact, be performed by different institutions, *functional alternatives*, depending upon the particular structural context in which they occur. Thus the integrative function of religion may be taken on by the state, or by the Communist Party in the context of Eastern Europe. For Merton, the concept of 'functional alternatives' was a means through which functionalists could be prevented from falling into the tautologous traps described earlier in the discussion of Malinowski and Radcliffe-Brown. In this way, what he regarded as one of functionalism's major problems, the danger of assuming that items must *always* fulfil system needs, would be avoided.

Thirdly, Merton introduced further refinements in the language of functional analysis. He pointed to the importance of considering *dysfunction* as well as *eufunction*; social practices could have adverse effects upon the social order as well as positive, integrative ones. Again, the structural context was of critical importance, and the particular function fulfilled by a social or cultural item a matter of empirical investigation. In some societies religion fulfils an integrative function. But in Northern Ireland, or in parts of the Middle East, it is clearly having the reverse effect. Merton emphasised that a particular element of culture or social practice could have a different effect at different levels of analysis. In these ways Merton attempted to revise and defend functionalism from its worst and most obvious weaknesses.

Talcott Parsons and structural functionalism

If Merton is remembered as the revisionist and defender of functionalism, it is his former teacher with whom the 'functionalism' of America in the mid-twentieth century is most associated. The writings of Talcott Parsons dominated American sociological theory from the end of the Second World War until the mid-1960s. But although it was widely influential, it was also widely criticised. It should also be recognised that there is some doubt as to whether Parsons, who is so identified with *structural functionalism*, can be classified as a functionalist at all. His early work, while being influenced by Durkheim, was also much influenced by Weber, and he claims it is a revision of 'action theory' which is discussed in the next chapter.

A number of students of Parsons' work have detected a gradual transformation in his writings, from the 'theory of action' in the 1930s to 'systems functionalism' in the 1960s and 1970s. While Parsons himself saw his work as developmental and cumulative within consistent principles, it is possible to differentiate between four distinct phases of it.

The first stage, in which he outlined the initial *'action–situation frame of reference'*, was based upon a systematic review of European social and economic thought, particularly that of Durkheim, Weber, Marshall and Pareto. The purpose of this review was to distil the key analytical ingredients necessary for the understanding of social action. Parsons' 'action–situation frame of reference' comprised the following components: actor, goal, orientation, situation. This basic model is anchored on the 'actor', through which Parsons intends to convey the importance of human choice and intentionality. But in his review of the work of Durkheim, Parsons clearly acknowledges the impact of 'social facts' and social forces in 'determining' social action. This is recognised in the significance of 'situation' in his basic theoretical model. Actors may choose courses of action, but in making 'orientations' they have to appreciate their 'situations', as well as the 'goals' they may wish to achieve. The 'actor–situation frame of reference' is then highly abstract but relatively simple.

The second phase of Parsons' work elaborated this basic framework and involved two complex and verbose treatises, *Towards a General Theory of Action* (written mainly with Edward Shils), and his own *The Social System* (both published in 1951). In these Parsons further refines his ideas on actors' 'orientations' and the ways in which different types of 'situations' influence the decisions we are likely to make. 'Orientations' are said to involve feelings (cathectic orientations) as well as cognitive and evaluative dimensions. To translate, as his critic Max Black did, Parsons 'discovered' that we think, feel and choose before we act.

Parson is, however, at pains to point out the ways in which the odds are stacked in favour of particular choices being taken in particular circumstances. Choices may be there, action may be entered into voluntarily, but there is a very important social structural context to that choice. One of the examples he outlines at some length, to illustrate this point, concerns medical practice. In choosing how to act towards a patient, a doctor does indeed have 'choices'. But the cultural paraphernalia of the surgery, and the training given to doctors, 'determine' the type of behaviour we expect and that which doctors are likely to 'choose' to follow. Parsons developed a complex schema for classifying choice patterns, known as the *'pattern variables'*. They are considered by him to be universally applicable, not only to individual actors but also to 'situations', institutions and social structures, where particular types of choice are to be expected (see Reading 4).

During the third stage of his work, Parsons concentrated on particular 'social sub-systems' and the connections between them. In the 1950s he was concerned with the interrelationship between the economy and the rest of society (*Economy and Society*, with Neil Smelser, 1956), and with the ways in which the family socialises members of a society, emotionally preparing them for the transition into a complex, highly structured world (*Family, Socialization and Interaction Process*, with Robert Bales, 1955). In the development of this aspect of Parsons' theory, the work of the social psychologist Robert Bales clearly influenced his thinking. Bales had studied small-group interaction in social psychology laboratories and, in particular, the kinds of difficulties groups faced in joint problem solving. For Parsons such problem solving was universal and occurred at the level of institutions and societies, as well as within small groups. A re-working of Bales's observations resulted in the *functional imperatives*. These specified the four 'problems' which must be 'solved' for any social group to survive and function adequately. The four functional imperatives, which became the linch-pin of all Parsons' future work, were *latency, integration, goal attainment and adaptation* (LIGA) (see Table 3.1).

Table 3.1 *Parsons' functional imperatives*

Adaptation	Goal attainment
Accommodation of the system to the demands and exigencies of the environment	Agreeing and defining objectives and priorities, and mobilising resources to ensure their realisation
(particularly associated with the problems of the economy in advanced societies)	(particularly associated with systems of power and organisation of government in advanced societies)

Latency	Integration
(Pattern maintenance and tension management)	Co-ordinating, organising and regulating relationships between members of a group or society in ways which afford legitimacy
Ensuring that members are broadly committed to societal or group values, and resolving strains and tensions between members in the expression of such commitment	(associated with education and the law in advanced societies)
(particularly associated with the family in advanced societies)	

During the 1950s Parsons concentrated upon integrating the pattern-variable framework, which classified choice patterns and *action*, with the LIGA framework, which classified the *functional requirements* of *social systems*. It is in this move from a theory of action to the analysis of the functioning of social systems that some scholars have seen a fundamental shift in Parsons' work.

In the fourth phase of his work, in the late 1950s, Parsons attempted to restructure his developing action/functional framework into a more complete and comprehensive theory. In particular, he concentrated upon specifying the internal workings of the four main 'systems of action' operating in society, and the ways in which these related together. These four main systems of action were the cultural system, the social system, the personality system and the organic system. This model was further elaborated in *Societies; Evolutionary and Comparative Perspectives* (1966). In particular Parsons tried to specify how 'cultures' (systems of ideas, beliefs and values) *'controlled'* society and through this the behaviour of individuals. In doing this he borrowed complex ideas from 'cybernetics' and 'systems theory' (see Table 3.2).

Table 3.2   Parsons' cybernetic model

Cultural system: ↑ ↓	system of ideas, beliefs, and values together with their symbolisation in knowledge, art, literature and other forms of representation.
Social system: ↓ ↑	system of patterns of normative expectations which become institutionalised within social structures. These were further specified into four 'levels of analysis': values, norms, collectivities and roles.
Personality system: ↓ ↑	system of relatively stable motives, predispositions and temperaments.
Organic system:	system of biological and psychological needs.

As he developed this model, Parsons began to turn his attention to the question which had figured prominently in the work of some of his nineteenth-century forebears – the question of evolution. Parsons' version referred to the ways in which evolution has taken place through the specialisation of particular institutions on 'sub-system' problems'. Such specialisation, or *'structural differentiation'* (leading to autonomous economic, political, legal, educational and family systems, for instance) had *adaptively upgraded* advanced industrial societies. This made them, Parsons claimed, increasingly capable of achieving material prosperity through specialisation and efficiency, while, at the same time, maintaining social unity, cohesion and consensus.

How do we evaluate functionalism?

It is difficult to know precisely how to evaluate functionalism because, as we have seen, many different formulations of it exist. The functionalism of Malinowski, with its emphasis on individual needs, is different from that of Radcliffe-Brown, with his more structural concerns. Similarly, Merton's arguments for an item-centred functionalism, calling as it did for empirically testable, *middle-range theories*, bears little resemblance to Parsons' structural functionalism, with its language of systems, cybernetics and heady abstraction. Indeed, Merton's call for theories of the middle range was a deliberate counterpoint to Parsons' drift towards stratospheric abstraction. To talk merely of 'functionalism' is to suggest a unity where it does not exist. Certainly there has been as much debate and argument *between* functionalists as there have been criticisms from those outside it.

The criticisms of functionalism have been far-reaching and are far too many in number to give them all proper consideration here. We have already mentioned its teleological tendencies. It has also been suggested that, as an approach, functionalism is, in fact, *descriptive* rather than providing theoretical explanations. It often provides a conceptual model which may *aid* understanding, without offering any detailed empirically-grounded theory of how or why particular aspects of society operate in the way they do. Some criticisms have centred on functionalism's limited and deficient analysis of human action – although Parsons claims to have been addressing this problem. Other functionalist theories, though, do produce models which are highly deterministic and mechanistic, conveying the image of individuals as controlled by factors external to them.

Other attacks on functionalism have focused on the consensual image of society which it portrays. Yet, in Parsons' formulation, it can be claimed that integration is posed as a *problem* to be dealt with, and not as something that is always necessarily and perfectly solved. What *is* absent, however, is any analysis of how *structured* conflict and division of interest occur and develop. Functionalists have described the functioning of the stratification system, but not the basic antagonisms of class; they have explored the division between male and female roles within the family as being functional for the efficient socialisation of children, but not the oppression of women privatised within the home; they have charted the evolution of 'citizenship for all' in modern society, but not the struggles against slavery, institutional racism and the persistence of prejudice. Functionalism has been more concerned with the theory of social order than with the reality of social inequalities. Whether this ideological conservativism is *logically* tied to the functionalist outlook is debatable. It can be pointed out, however, that from Comte, to Durkheim, to Parsons, the terminology of functionalism has appeared in conjunction with a rejection of radical politics.

Finally, it must be emphasised that not only self-acclaimed 'functionalists' employ what has been described here as the functionalist approach. Elements of functionalism can be found within Marxism. For example, the terminology of functionalism is used to explain how certain kinds of values and ideas coalesce into types of ideologies which are regarded as functional to the maintenance of the capitalist system. In a similar way, certain feminists have analysed the nuclear family in terms of how it supports both the capitalistic economic system and male dominance. The language of functionalism is implicit here, but the outcome in terms of analysis is largely the same. Yet Marxists and feminists have been some of the most outspoken critics of the functionalist view. It is clearly necessary to guard against slipping unwittingly into 'functionalist-speak'

Functionalism and positivism

In the literature on sociological theory functionalism is often treated as a form of positivism, or positivism is treated as the methodological instrument of functionalism. Yet the two cannot be equated in this simplistic fashion. For a start, much functional analysis is not presented in a propositional form such that it could be empirically tested. For a period of forty or so years, for instance, Parsons was constantly berated for not making explicit the relationship between his theoretical enterprise and the 'nitty gritty' of empirical research (although he himself claimed that empirical propositions were deducible from his work). Functionalism, in the main, has been about looking for universally applicable functions and developing analytical frameworks. This is not the same as establishing positivistic general laws.

Despite this, it has to be acknowledged that the functionalist approach was generated in the nineteenth century by the same thinkers who emphasised the importance of positivism and sociology's similarity with the natural sciences. However, whereas positivism has gone on to emphasise the scientific, methodological and, subsequently, the deductive aspects of scientific thought, functionalism has its roots in a slightly different focus – one which concentrates on understanding evolution and treating society as an organism (the biological analogy). Although originating from the same concern, these emphases cannot be reduced to each other. The two, with all their variations, must be kept separate and distinct if we are to comprehend both their ambitions and the difficulties they reveal about the business of theory construction.

4 Interpretivism and the importance of meaning

The interpretivist perspective in sociology is usually regarded as the direct opposite of functionalist and positivist approaches. The latter, as we have seen, try to analyse the social world in ways similar to those used in the natural sciences, although there are differences in how this is conceived. Interpretivists, however, see a fundamental difference in studying society. The difference lies in the fact that, whereas the natural sciences deal with a physical, inanimate world, the social sciences are concerned with areas of life where people think, and have ideas and beliefs which guide their actions. For this reason interpretivists hold that *meaning* should be the cornerstone of any sociological theory. The significance of meaning has, however, varying consequences for different interpretivists. Paradoxically, different branches of interpretivism mean different things by 'meaning'. Some of these differences will be explored in this chapter.

Weber and *'Verstehen'*

The work of Max Weber (1864–1920) is often portrayed as being a continuous dialogue with the ghost of Marx. In the book *The Protestant Ethic and the Spirit of Capitalism* (1920), for example, he took issue with what he felt to be Marx's over-emphasis on materialist or economic factors in historical development generally, but particularly in the genesis of capitalism. His analysis of social stratification in terms of class, status and power was similarly designed to undermine Marx's claim that social divisions were solely economic in nature. In these and other areas of his work, Weber was trying to rectify what he saw as a neglect of subjective factors in Marx's writings. Although Weber was a prolific writer who was interested in a wide range of social matters, from religion to inequality, from bureaucracy to comparative analysis, it is his focus on meaning which concerns us here.

For Weber, the basis of sociology was societal beliefs and the meanings individuals give to the social world and their situation in it. This meant that sociology was a different kind of enterprise from that undertaken by the natural sciences. One of the major differences between them was that sociology had to employ 'Verstehen', empathetic understanding, in order to reveal how beliefs and motives lead to particular actions and behaviour. For Weber, we do not have to be sympathetic to the beliefs (believe them ourselves). Rather, we should think of ourselves as in the place of the believer, so that we can appreciate the cognitive and motivational implications of holding particular beliefs.

Weber distinguishes between two kinds of meaning. *Direct observational understanding* refers to the kind of understanding you have when you see $2 + 2 = 4$. The proposition is understood in terms of its own internal logic. *Explanatory understanding* is the one which is vital for sociology. It is the meaning we have when we interpret $2 + 2 = 4$, knowing that, for example, it is being used in the context of balancing some accounts. Here we understand it as part of an action in which the actor has particular *purposes or intentions*. In other words, our understanding is derived from our interpretation as to how an actor is defining the situation which she or he is in.

Weber argued that sociological explanations have to be evaluated in two different ways. Firstly, they have to be *'adequate at the level of meaning'*. This involves showing that actions which are the focus of sociological concern are 'meaningful' – that is, make sense as the outcomes of human agency. Secondly, explanations should also be *'causally adequate'*. This refers to the need to establish causal connections between occurrences. In *The Protestant Ethic and the Spirit of Capitalism*, for instance, Weber employs this two-pronged approach. He used *'Verstehen'* to understand the meaning of Calvinist beliefs and appreciate what these meant in terms of action in industry and the economy. He also demonstrated the existence of a correlation between Calvinists' beliefs and capitalism. He could then claim that it was the existence of these Protestant views which had caused capitalism to develop.

There are two significant points about how Weber's sociology deals with meaning. Firstly, Weber *infers* meaning on the basis of indirect evidence. In *The Protestant Ethic*, for instance, he draws out the meaning of Protestant beliefs on the basis of reading historical documents, diaries and religious texts. Weber uses these to *reconstruct* meaning. He is not directly concerned with the views of the individuals themselves. Secondly, when he discusses meaning, Weber does not include every belief of Protestantism or every aspect of capitalism. Rather, he selects those elements which seem to him to be the most relevant to the phenomena he is investigating. This is the basis of one of his special tools for constructing sociological meaning: the *ideal type*.

An ideal type is constructed by abstracting and combining a number of characteristics of a phenomenon which, although found in reality, are rarely or never discovered in this special 'ideal' form. Hence Weber's terminology for them: 'ideal' or 'pure' types. Ideal types are deliberate, one-sided accentuations of particular features of a phenomenon. They are simply shorthand ways of making sense of complex aspects of the social world. They are not supposed to be replications of them.

Weber constructed different kinds of ideal types which operate at different levels of sociological analysis. For instance, he classified different types of action in terms of the kinds of meaning the action had for the actor: action directed to the achievement of one overriding goal (*Wertrationalitat*); action in which a number of possible goals are weighed up and balanced and the appropriate means of achieving them selected (*Zweckrationalitat*); action derived from the obligations and expectations laid down by tradition and custom (*traditional action*); action resulting from states or feelings of emotion (*affectual action*). Weber goes on to use these types of action as the basis for classifying types of society and social organisation.

Despite the fact that some aspects of Weber's work are still used in contemporary research (for example, the work of John Rex on race and the use of 'status' in stratification studies), his theoretical work on meaning has been subject to critical review. For example, his construction of ideal types makes no attempt to be historically accurate. The typology of *The Protestant Ethic* is derived from diaries and writings (of Benjamin Franklin, for instance) which are taken from a period well beyond the onset of capitalism and from outside of Western Europe. Although Franklin may be 'exemplary' of the subjectivity Weber wishes to portray, should we not expect his views to be accurately conveyed? Apparently not. Weber's method allowed him full liberty to use, select and abstract whatever he chose in order to construct his ideal type. This indicates that, although he was interested in actors' meanings, for Weber it was primarily the sociologist who determined what these meanings should be. It was these difficulties, with ideal types and meaning, which formed the main targets for his critic Alfred Schutz, to whom we will turn next.

Phenomenology and Schutz

Alfred Schutz (1899–1959) was a German theorist who went to America as a European refugee in the 1930s. However, his major book, *The Phenomenology of the Social World*, was not translated into English until the 1960s. At this time the dominance of structural functionalism was being attacked, and sociologists were searching for new theoretical ideas and approaches. Schutz's work became of critical importance in this endeavour.

Phenomenology is a way of looking at the social world which asks us *not* to take things for granted. At all times, in all societies and cultures, each new generation is taught how to conceive of things, and this teaching is central to socialisation. This means that we are brought up to understand the world and its parts in certain ways, ways we take for granted or think of as 'natural'. Phenomenology asks us to question our very basic assumptions about the world. It asks us to focus on the common-sense aspects of our culture, particularly those which make up our ordinary, or as Schutz would say, 'everyday' world. Phenomenology was originally a strand of philosophical thinking. It was Schutz who developed it in ways which showed its potential for sociology.

Schutz agrees with Weber that the essential role of social science is to be *interpretive* – that is, to understand the subjective meaning of social action. However, he argues that Weber failed to state clearly how this was to be achieved. In particular, Weber failed to make clear the essential characteristics of understanding, subjective meaning and action. He also ignored the fact that there are different kinds of understanding, meaning and action. Weber's imprecision is so serious to Schutz that it significantly weakens the foundations of interpretive sociology. The concept of subjective meaning is so ambiguous in Weber's work that it is not clear whether the point of view to be sought is that of the actors themselves or that of the sociological observer. Weber also failed to bring out the *inter-subjective* nature of the social world. For Schutz the everyday world is inter-subjective because it is shared. It is not a 'private' world, personal to each individual, but one in which we continually interact with others and interpret their actions.

Schutz was also critical of Weber's use of the ideal type. He claimed that it was not clear how the ideal type, which is supposed to be scientific and objective, can be used to understand the subjective meaning of individuals.

In Schutz's view three interrelated types of enquiry are necessary for a phenomenology of the social world. The first is a clarification of the basic concepts involved, especially those of 'subjective meaning', 'action' and 'inter-subjectivity'. The second is the development of distinctions and categories to help in understanding the dynamics and structure of the world of everyday life. For example, the concept of *stock of common-sense knowledge* refers to knowledge of the world which all social actors possess. This knowledge is essentially *practical*. It is acquired by actors in the process of living and coping with the situations and experiences they encounter. Knowledge is also *'socially distributed'*. Although elements of it are shared with others, each individual has different kinds and amounts depending on his or her own personal history and experience. Schutz also introduces the term *'multiple realities'*. This means that there are several orders of reality, each with its own special and separate style of existence – for instance, the world of dreams, of science, of religion, as well as the everyday world. Any attempt to change from one to the other jolts an individual's understanding because it involves changing from one style of lived experience to another.

The third step in developing a phenomenological sociology is, according to Schutz, formulating a scientific method for generating theories. Here he differentiates between *first-* and *second-order constructs*. First-order constructs are the typifications used by ordinary actors. These are created from their common-sense knowledge and used to define the world and guide their actions in it. Second-order constructs are ideal types constructed by the sociologist on the basis of observing the first-order constructs of people. They are therefore based on actors' typifications but go beyond them in the sense that they are more general and have greater explanatory power. The second-order meanings are generated from first-order meanings.

Schutz sets out three scientific postulates which must be met when developing second-order constructs. *The postulate of logical consistency* implies that the construct must make sense to other sociologists who might use it. *The postulate of subjective interpretation* requires that the construct explains the subjective meaning any observed actions might have for the actors concerned. *The postulate of adequacy* demands that if an act, as typified by the construct, were performed in real life, it would be understandable both by the actor and by those with whom she or he was interacting.

A number of criticisms of phenomenology have been advanced. For instance, it has been said that in concentrating so much on meaning, it is unable to explore social structures and how they arise and are sustained. Marxists, such as Adorno and Marcuse, have accused phenomenology of being both ahistorical and uncritical of the form the social world takes. Not only does the phenomenological world appear unchanging; it is also impervious to issues such as those of inequality or power. Schutz's emphasis on *observation* of action as a way of getting to grips with actors' meanings can also be criticised. As with Weber, this involves Schutz offering *his* interpretation of actors' meanings, even at the first-order level, rather than, for example, asking for their understandings and views directly. Some commentators have also suggested that Schutz's model is so complex that it is difficult to see how it could be actually used.

Yet, although Schutz did not engage in any empirical work himself, phenomenology has had a tremendous influence on certain areas of sociology – in, for example, the study of education and deviance (see Reading 5). In deviance it led, for instance, to a questioning of criminal statistics and of the taken-for-granted assumptions used in constructing them. In education, sociologists have used phenomenology to look at how common-sense assumptions structure classroom interaction and lead certain pupils to be 'typed' as failures because of this. In these sorts of ways, phenomenology has been responsible for opening up for scrutiny a whole range of areas which had been overlooked, or simply taken for granted, in previous sociological work. For this reason its influence on sociology in recent years has been highly significant.

Ethnomethodology

Ethnomethodology grew out of the work of Schutz, but it is different from it in many ways. Like phenomenology, ethnomethodology regards social organisation as something which is constructed out of the interaction of individuals. However, whereas Schutz would argue that order is the result of shared common-sense knowledge, ethnomethodology argues that such knowledge is itself variable and is something which is created anew in each encounter. Whereas Schutz argued that interaction takes place because actors assume that they hold similar assumptions, ethno-methodologists claim that these assumptions have to be 'worked at' all the time. Every piece of social interaction is regarded as a practical achievement, as something 'done' or 'accomplished'. Ethnomethodologists seek to find out how it is done. Hence its name. Ethnomethodology is concerned with the study of (-ology) ordinary people's (ethno) methods for making sense of and creating order in everyday life.

Ethnomethodology starts out from a criticism of all other forms of established sociology. This is usually stated by saying that sociology takes as a 'resource' what in fact should be a 'topic' of study. The familiar common-sense world of meanings, shared by sociologist and non-sociologist alike, is employed in an unques-tioning way in sociological analysis. It is this taken-for-granted meaningfulness in sociology, as well as in the ordinary world, which ethnomethodologists wish to explore. In general, ethno-methodologists try to avoid simply adopting the explanations and accounts of lay persons in their work. Rather, they take them as the object of their study.

There are a number of aspects of ethnomethodology which require emphasis. These derive from the work of Harold Garfinkel, who is usually taken to be the founder of the approach (see Reading 6). The first of these is the idea of the indexicality of meaning. By this is meant that the vast majority of expressions and terms in language have meanings which alter depending on the context in which they are used. Their precise sense is only settled by looking at the situation in which they are being uttered. For ethnomethodology, when people talk or act they are constantly engaged in interpreting what is going on around them. We use our knowledge and understanding of other people constantly to re-define and re-evaluate what is going on. Even producing relatively smooth conversation and interaction is a highly skilled art which only appears to be so natural and unprob-lematic because we are so practised at it.

A second significant feature of ethnomethodology is the notion of *reflexivity*. This underlines the inherent relationship between talk and action. When we describe a situation we are, at the same time, creating it and making it occur. Another way of describing this is to say that 'talk is not merely *about* actions, events and situations, it is also a potent and *constituent part of* those actions, events and situations' (J. Potter and M. Wetherell, *Discourse and Social Psychology*, Sage, 1987). Part of the ethnomethodological endeavour is to discover how reality is put together and defined through taken-for-granted rules. Note: it is not rules in the normative and prescriptive sense usually meant by sociologists which are referred to here. Such rules are portrayed as guides to behaviour, which actors passively follow. Rather, ethnomethodological rules help to construct not only action but also the meaning of that action.

Ethnomethodologists' approach to rules constitutes a third significant element of their particular focus, for they claim that rules are never applied in a strict or absolute fashion. Instead, it is always necessary to elaborate on a rule before it can be used, and the kind of elaboration needed will depend upon the circumstances to hand. This is what Garfinkel refers to as the *etcetera clause*. It allows novel or unforeseen circumstances to be included in the rubric of a rule and for a certain degree of flexibility in its usage.

During the 1970s, when ethnomethodologists were developing their approach, it tended to be treated with hostility by many sociologists. They regarded it either as trivial or as trying to undermine all other existing forms of sociology. Many criticisms of ethnomethodology were voiced. For example, it was claimed that ethnomethodology had no set methods for acquiring knowledge and no criteria for evaluating the variety that it used. As one writer, Alun Blum, put it: 'One just gets the hang of it.' Ethnomethodology was also challenged for its apparent 'indifference' as to whether its activities and subject matter were significant areas for academic pursuit. It was chided for its apparent lack of social or political concern.

A further criticism was that ethnomethodology offered no criteria for choosing between different members' accounts of situations. Each account had the same weight or significance as any other. There was no objective way of evaluating them. In addition, it was pointed out that the ethnomethodologists' emphasis on things like indexicality and reflexivity led them to a *relativist* position. From their point of view there was no 'real' world comprised of definitive institutions and structures. Instead, all that existed were interactive individuals creating and re-creating meaning. Whereas Schutzian phenomenology had been concerned to construct theoretical understandings and expla-nations of the social world, ethnomethodology was hardly concerned with theorising at all. Rather, it seemed to focus on a never-ending string of events. The result was simply descrip-tions, but these were never used to construct theory. In this sense Z. Bauman (*Sociological Review*, 1973) argued that ethnometho-dology was a form of positivism, committed only to collecting facts.

In recent years, however, ethnomethodologists' interest in the taken-for-granted has become more integrated and accepted into the general sociological enterprise. Different kinds of ethnometh-odology have developed. Probably the best-known formulation in the 1980s is *conversational analysis* (CA). As Potter and Wetherell have described it, CA focuses on everyday talk and the way different types of action – such as blamings, greetings and excuses – are produced (*Discourse and Social Psychology*, Sage, 1987). It regards conversational exchanges between people as playing a crucial part in the creation of their social world and how they understand it. It is *how* people talk which is of interest to CA.

Typically, analysts concentrate on the minutiae of conversations as conducted by ordinary people and recorded in verbatim tran-scripts (including the timing of pauses). The assumption is that talk is organised and that this is achieved by those doing the talking. The organisation or orderliness of talk becomes apparent by examining many examples of the same kind of talk. The immediate aim of CA is to uncover the hidden and underlying form or structure of conversations. As studies accumulate, it is hoped that it might be possible to describe in general 'the elab-orate and detailed architecture of conversation'.

Symbolic interactionism

Symbolic interactionism comprised the major alternative form of sociology to functionalism and Parsonianism in America in the first half of this century. But despite its undoubted influence, it is extraordinarily difficult to pin down precisely. Not all of the writers who tend to be bracketed together under this label necessarily approve of the term. Sometimes the name 'interactionist' or 'the Chicago School' is used instead. Sometimes the 'dramaturgical approach' of Erving Goffman is included under the symbolic interactionist heading.

Blumer has summarised the major aspects of symbolic interaction in three major tenets (see Table 4.1) The most important emphasis is upon the *symbolic universe* in which human beings live. We are both inhabitants and the creators of a world comprising language, symbols and gestures. These enable us to attach meaning to objects and actions in everyday life, to interpret the world around us and daily to create social life. It is this symbolic world of meanings which marks us off from the animal world. Our ability to make and manipulate symbols is what makes us truly human and social.

Table 4.1   Herbert Blumer's three tenets of symbolic interaction

1   Human beings act towards things on the basis of the meanings that these have for them.

2   These meanings are the product of social interaction in human society.

3   These meanings are handled in, and modified through, an interpretive process that is used by each individual in dealing with the things each encounters.

For symbolic interactionists meanings arise out of interaction and not the other way round. Human beings act towards others and objects on the basis of the meanings that such things have for them, but meanings are always being modified and constructed through interaction. Meanings, therefore, remain constantly negotiable. Whenever a person enters any social situation, many processes come into play. The person has to indicate to herself what she is expected to do, how she would like to be seen, what 'meanings' the objects in her path have, what meanings other actors in the situation are attributing to her and themselves, and so on. This process is known as '*the definition of the situation*'. It is only possible through the symbolic use of language, and meaning attribution.

A further basic premiss of symbolic interactionism is that individuals can never be considered in isolation from their interactive partners – actual or ideal, real or imaginary. The centrality of this 'otherness' is reflected in some of the key concepts of symbolic interactionists like 'self', 'role', 'reference group', 'significant other'. Even the 'self' is social in character. Mead divided it into the 'I' and the 'me'. The 'me' is myself as others see me. The 'I' is that part of me that looks at myself. The self is constructed through constant interplay between the 'I' and the 'me'. Any human activity involves an individual, not just acting, but 'imaginatively' anticipating the responses of others to that action. The 'I' is the source of freedom in action. The 'me' gives it some stability. Overall, the 'I' and the 'me' which comprise the self provide a constant link between the individual and society.

The 'self' and the social formation of 'identities' have been the basis for much research work carried out by symbolic interactionists in the fields of mental illness, deviancy and the sociology of education. In particular they have explored the ways in which identities, images and the behaviour associated with these are developed in and through social interaction. 'Labelling' theory and the concept of deviant 'career' are examples of two developments in sociology which have emerged from this kind of work (see Reading 7).

Many of the criticisms directed at symbolic interactionism are similar to those made of phenomenology. For example, it is said to be ahistorical and to ignore the wider features of social structure, so that it cannot say anything about power, conflict and social change. It is also accused of presenting too self-conscious and rational a picture of individuals, who appear logical and unemotional in choosing how to act. Like ethnomethodology it is chided for being too vague theoretically and for not providing a more integrated conceptual framework. However, although at first sight symbolic interactionism may appear fairly similar to ethnomethodology, there are important differences between them.

Symbolic interactionists assume the prior existence of a symbolic order and language structure, and use these to explore meaning negotiation and interaction. For ethnomethodologists the very existence of such order and language structure is an accomplishment and cannot be assumed. It is precisely these aspects of social organisation, which symbolic interactionists take for granted, that ethnomethodologists wish to investigate. Whereas ethnomethodologists concentrate upon the invisible, taken-for-granted processes which make meaning itself possible, symbolic interactionists look at how different meanings are negotiated. Ethnomethodology assumes that the individual is unaware of how meaning is constructed. Symbolic interactionism always starts and finishes from the 'actors' point of view'.

Conclusion

It should be clear from the above discussion that there are several differences of approach to be found among those sociologists who are usually put together in the interpretivist camp. Firstly, there is a difference in the kind of meaning referred to. Some writers simply focus on the sociologists' interpretations, while others wish to include, in some way, actors' accounts.

A second variation lies in the sociological uses to which the analyses of meaning are put. While writers like Weber want to use them to build up general theories, others – ethnomethodologists, for example – are more concerned to describe hidden structures than to theorise at all. A third difference relates to the ways in which research is conducted.

For Weber, the main strategy was the reconstruction of meaning using ideal types, based upon the study of historical documents and secondary sources.

CA uses more technically precise methods of data collection, such as tape and video recorders.

Only symbolic interactionists, together with some phenomenologists, advocate the use of participant observation in the belief that participation is an important strategy for discovering the definitions and meanings being used in everyday life. Yet participant observation is *the* method usually associated with interpretive theorising. This is despite the fact that participant observation can take many forms and is more properly considered to be a general approach than a distinctive methodological practice. It has also been used by positivists and functional anthropologists.

Interpretive sociology therefore comprises an array of different approaches to sociological understanding in which a variety of different research methods are used. If it can be regarded as some sort of intellectual alliance, this has more to do with its united opposition to positivism than any real unity of principle or practice.

5 Marx and Marxism

For more than a century there has been a close but uneasy and contentious relationship between Marxism and sociology. They have been close because Marx's theory, like sociology, was intended to be a general science of society, directed particularly towards understanding those changes which had resulted from industrial capitalism. At the same time, unease and contention have arisen because Marxism and sociology have developed in largely separate intellectual circles and because of the controversy as to whether Marxism is just one sociological theory among others, or whether it is a unique body of thought which exists as a radical alternative to sociology. All this is further confused by the many varied interpretations of both Marx's writings and those of his successors. Not only is there disagreement as to what Marx 'really' said, there is also dispute over Marxists' interpretations of Marx, as well as argument over the most useful ways in which his thinking might be developed.

One particular bone of contention has been over whether a change of direction occurs in Marx's thinking. Louis Althusser has argued that after about 1845 there is a break in Marx's work which separates the young 'humanist' writer influenced by the philosopher Hegel, from the mature thinker who created a rigorous economic science of society. This view is not easy to sustain, especially when the content and argument of Marx's later writings are compared with the earlier texts. It is more plausible to suggest that, having first sketched the general outline of his theory, Marx then turned to a more detailed and thorough analysis of the capitalist mode of production. Both of these were necessary to his overall aim – that of developing a theory of the process of social development which would show how capitalism would be superseded.

Marx's theoretical approach

Although commentators have referred to Marx's 'historical' and 'dialectical materialism', he himself never used these terms, preferring instead '*the materialist conception of history*'. This outlined the idea that the essential element in the understanding of human history is productive activity or *labour*. History is the (mostly unconscious) creation of labouring men who create it in the process of trying to obtain subsistence, or make a living, for themselves and their families. In this sense, then, labour is the primary factor in history and of greater significance than ideas. Marx's materialism meant, quite simply, that the starting point for analysing society should always be the *material conditions of production* – the circumstances under which labour is organised and things are produced.

Marx was aware that human actors do not freely create the society which is the product of their labour, because they are always limited by the historical circumstances in which they find themselves, the foundations of which have been laid by previous generations. However, he did not believe that humans are completely *determined* by such circumstances. Rather, at particular points in history, the material conditions which frame our existence are conducive to change. At such points, providing they fully understand that they can be agents of social change, human beings are able to transform the nature of society. Marx called this *praxis* (the unity of theory and practice). In praxis we have the notion that only *people* can alter the shape of history. It does not change of its own accord.

Two other aspects of Marx's theoretical approach should also be mentioned at this point. The first is that it is not an empirical theory; that is, Marx did not believe that insights could be derived purely by collecting facts. He drew a distinction between *essence* and *appearance*. In this Marx contended that the essence of something is never what it actually appears to be. We should never take things at face value but should always probe for underlying characteristics and structures. For instance, the relationship between capitalist and worker might appear, at first sight, to be fair and rational. Marx was able to point to critical aspects which lay beneath surface appearances which highlighted their irrational and exploitative elements.

Marx also made a distinction between the *real* and the *ideal*. For Marx the real is always striving to become the ideal. Some phenomena are always in the process of becoming something other than they appear to be. For instance, Marx's view of human nature was expressed, as we shall see, in terms of how it *ought* to be, rather than as it really was at a particular moment in history. He regarded nineteenth-century humans, dominated and oppressed by the social system, as imperfect, flawed examples of what they could be: the ideal. Marx was interested in the socio-economic conditions which would make this ideal attainable for everyone.

Species-being and alienation

In his early work Marx emphasised two particular concepts: species-being and alienation. Species-being refers to what makes the life of the human species different from that of animals – that the faculties, capacities and tasks of humans are shaped by society. Being a member of society confers 'humanity' on us. It generates the possibility that collective activity, through socially organised labour, can be used for the collective good. But in capitalist society, according to Marx, humans are *estranged* from the ties which make them human. This is because under capitalism the separate needs of competing individuals 'appear' to exist independently of, and be more important than membership of, society. This form of distortion is referred to as 'alienation'. Because society constrains our existence, human beings are alienated from nature, from themselves, from their species-being and from other human beings.

Alienation occurs when human beings find their activities, their 'essence', operating on them as an external, alien and oppressive power. Under capitalism our 'self-confirming essence', labour, is increasingly turned against us. Work becomes a forced activity, which instead of being fulfilling, stunts imagination and induces misery, exhaustion and mental despair. Work becomes instrumental, rather than an activity for itself and in its own right. This alienation of the worker in the capitalist economy is founded upon the disparity between the increasingly productive power of labour and the lack of control which workers can exert over their lives. They become indispensable cogs in a machine producing goods which they do not own and may not even need or want. Alienation is, then, clearly linked to the structure of the capitalist economic system.

Alienation, with its description of humans as wrenched from

their essential being and purpose in life, is crucial to an understanding of Marx's thought. It underlies all his later work, which
was designed to explicate further the socio-economic conditions
of capitalist society and the circumstances under which they might
be challenged.

The relations of production and the class structure

In developing his materialist model of society Marx distinguished
between the 'real' foundation or the '*base*', and the '*superstructure*'.
The base comprises the means of production (the ways in which
a particular society produces goods) and the relations of
production (comprising the social relationships between individuals, or class relations). The superstructure develops from
these two basic relationships through which material production
takes place. It is made up of a society's legal and political framework, and forms of social consciousness (values, ideologies,
scientific systems – in other words, all forms of thought) (see
Reading 8).

Marx argued that every kind of productive system generates a
definite set of social relationships between those individuals
involved in the productive process. Under capitalism these are
class relations. Classes emerge where the division of labour is such
that it allows for surpluses to be produced and accumulated. The
surpluses are appropriated and taken into ownership by one
particular group, who use them in their own interests to generate
further surpluses and wealth for themselves. Classes are, then,
based on the ownership and non-ownership of property. Those
who do not own property have no means of providing for themselves other than selling their *labour power*. This they do to the
owning class in conditions of exploitation. The owning class is
also the *ruling class*, because its economic power also gives it the
control of politics and of the system of beliefs and ideas. It is
therefore able to create ideas and disseminate them. These ideas,
the *dominant ideology*, contain sentiments which legitimate and
justify the system of class domination. They offer a distorted view
of the world which permeates the thinking of the non-owning
classes, so that their consciousness becomes *false consciousness*.

Because classes are constituted through the relationship that
individuals have to the means of production in society, Marx's

model of class is usually regarded as being dichotomous. The *bourgeoisie* (owners) and the *proletariat* (workers) are presented as two antagonistic classes, in a relationship of domination, sub-ordination and conflict. It must be emphasised, however, that the model of a dichotomous class system is only a theoretical construction in Marx's writings. It is a system to which bourgeois society is moving, rather than one which actually exists. All existing and previous class societies have a more complicated system of overlapping relationships (see Reading 9).

Marx made the important distinction between a *'class in itself'* and a *'class for itself'*. A 'class in itself' simply has a definite relationship to the means of production. The individuals involved neither identify with one another nor have a shared consciousness about their class position. A 'class for itself' occurs when its members are so conscious of their similar position and class interests that this becomes the basis for action. For Marx, when the proletariat became a 'class for itself', it would be transformed into an active force, capable of bringing about social change.

The theory of capitalist development

It is in Marx's theory of capitalist development that the previously discussed aspects of his model come together. He saw capitalism as a system of *exploitation*, but at the same time he recognised that it contained within it the seeds of its own destruction. Capitalism was built upon *contradictions*.

In his discussion of exploitation Marx provided part of his explanation as to how capitalist economics worked. He distinguished between *use value* and *exchange value*. Use value refers to the needs which a particular commodity can fulfil. *Exchange value* is the value a product has when exchanged for other products. When a worker sells his or her labour power at work (s)he receives a wage from the employer in return. This wage is always less than the sum for which the employer can sell the commodity which the worker has produced. The worker therefore creates extra value for the capitalist. Because the capitalist owns the productive system this *surplus value* or *profit* belongs to him. The capitalist class thus derives its social and economic advantages largely through the toil of others. This is exploitation, for Marx, because it involves treating workers as mere units in the productive process, as 'things' or as commodities whose labour power will be bought or not depending on its price (the wage). It is also exploitative because of the vast difference between the value of wages and that of profits, and because of the alienating circumstances of work.

In Marx's view the never-ending and intensifying search for profit was an inevitable part of capitalism. But, at the same time, there was rooted in the capitalist economy an economic law which would lead the rate of profit to decline. This was because capitalists were continually 'cutting their own throats'. They needed to make a profit, but to do this they also needed to compete with other capitalists. To do this they tried to capture a larger share of the market by reducing the price of their commodities. But this solution was precarious, since others were likely to follow suit. Another solution was to cut wages, but this also generated problems because capitalists are dependent upon workers having a reasonable standard of living so that they can buy the things that they themselves make. Marx saw all this as leading to recurrent economic crises. He regarded this as part of the *contradictions* or conflicts that are built into the structure of the capitalist economy (see Reading 10).

Marx clearly saw the capitalist system as doomed to failure. The contradictions within it would intensify, leading to more acute crises and economic difficulties. But although its demise was part of the internal logic of capitalism itself, a new system would not *automatically* emerge from it. Rather, as we saw earlier, Marx believed that humans make their own history. It was necessary for people to *want* a better society and to *act* to bring it about. It is the proletariat who, under the right circumstances, would be able to do this. Once changing economic circumstances intensified, they would be able to see through the dominant ideology, which supported their exploitation, and throw off their false consciousness. The proletariat would then become a class for itself. It would develop into a truly revolutionary grouping, fighting to overthrow the exploitative and alienating system of capitalist production and seizing for itself the ownership of the means of production, which could then be turned to more humane use.

Responses to Marx

Marx's theory has come under attack from virtually every intellectual tradition. It has been accused of ignoring improved standards of living which have blurred class divisions, of predicting a revolution which has not occurred, of offering no clear blueprint of what a socialist society would be like, of presenting political doctrinism rather than social analysis. These and other criticisms are well known.

Less frequently documented in textbooks are the debates which have subsequently arisen within Marxism, as writers have struggled to develop and extend Marx's framework. These debates are interesting, from the point of view of this book, because they once again point to differences of opinion and approach within a perspective which is frequently presented as homogeneous. Although many Marxist orientations have developed, two will be the focus of discussion here, the critical theory of the Frankfurt School and the work of Althusser. These have been chosen to illustrate the extreme range of thinking that now exists in Marxist writings. Whereas the Frankfurt School starts from the assumption that society is composed of human beings who think, feel and act, Althusser is concerned with structures. Another way of summarising the distinction between the two is that critical theory is 'humanist' while Althusserian theory is 'structuralist'.

The Frankfurt School of critical theory

The Frankfurt Institute for Social Research was founded in 1923. A number of well-known intellectuals were associated with the school, but the three main figures were Theodor Adorno, Max Horkheimer and Herbert Marcuse. All are now dead. With the rise of Hitler, all the members of the School were driven into exile in the USA. Adorno and Horkheimer eventually returned to Germany. Marcuse remained in the States. Although there were differences in the thinking of the three, there are sufficient similarities between them for common themes to be drawn out.

The Frankfurt School held the position that human beings should be able to change their social world positively because they have the ability to be critical of it and act on the basis of this critique. In this they were heavily influenced by the writings of the early Marx in his Hegelian phase. However, the school claimed that the Marxism of their day was unable to take account of this transformatory potential in individuals. There were a number of reasons for this. Firstly, Marxism had become too *economistic*. By this they meant that it overemphasised economic forces and factors as determining individual action. It was also over-concerned with setting out economic laws that were likely to lead to social change. The consequence of both of these was that the role of individual actors themselves was played down. Secondly, the school criticised Marxists for giving insufficient attention to the fact that capitalism had not been overthrown, as their theory predicted. Instead, the proletariat, supposedly the revolutionary class, had conspired in and supported the development of fascism and the Nazi regime in Europe. Yet Marxism seemed neither interested in this, nor able to explain it. The reason for this lack of concern, thirdly, was that, in concentrating so much on the economic, Marxists had ignored the superstructure. They had failed to provide analyses of ideology, culture and consciousness. The Frankfurt School argued that capitalism had changed since Marx's day so that ideological forces were now much more important. A central question for them was, why had the working classes been 'bought off' by capitalism and by what means had they been integrated into the capitalist system? The concepts of 'instrumental reason', 'mass culture' and 'domination' were developed to explain this.

Instrumental reason is, according to critical theorists, the dominant way of thinking in the modern world. It is concerned only with practical purposes and with means rather than ends. Issues dealing with meaning or the ultimate worth of actions cannot be countenanced. Everything is dealt with in as efficient, rational and logical way as possible. There is no room for questioning this efficiency and rationality. There is no space for asking why we are doing this or what it is for.

In his book *One Dimensional Man*, Marcuse points to the irrationality to which such a system leads. For instance, capitalist society has increased its scientific knowledge and productivity hugely in the twentieth century. But how are these gains used? Under instrumental reason science is used to create weapons of mass destruction which have the capacity to blow up the entire world. Although most people in the Western world now enjoy a reasonable standard of living, they are continually encouraged to want more, rather than to criticise a society which encourages continual conspicuous consumption. For Marcuse, this is a society without values or a social conscience – instrumental reason has no reason. It should be noted that critical theorists regarded positivist sociology as an example of instrumental reason (see Reading 11).

Individuals' acceptance of instrumental reason, their integration into society and their lack of critical thinking is explained by the Frankfurt School in terms of the development of *mass culture* and the mass media. These represent major changes in the development of capitalism to its organisation in Marx's day. Not only is culture now an industry and part of big business, but developments in technology have meant that, through newspapers, the cinema, radio (and now television and videos), it reaches the mass of the population. The Frankurt School regard mass culture as stultifying the population and as making them into passive recipients of whatever is 'dished out'. An audience is not required to make any effort to understand the content of mass culture. It simply soaks it up in an uncritical fashion. This kind of 'entertainment' lulls people into a false acceptance of the society in which they live. It stifles criticism, political challenge and conflict.

Marcuse talks about the way in which the culture industry produces and satisfies *'false needs'*. A 'true' need is one which, if satisfied, enables an individual to extend control over his or her life and enrich his or her relationships with others. A 'false' need is one created by mass culture; for example, the 'need' for a new record, the latest video, a foreign holiday. Such 'needs' emphasise the individual rather than the collective good. They can only be provided by the culture industry itself and thus they promote and support that industry. Their aim and their achievement are to lock people into the *'domination'* of the consumption society. Consuming mass culture dominates our lives.

The final element of the Frankfurt School theory is its examination of the process through which the *domination* of mass culture enters into the very heart of the individual. Much use is made of psychoanalytic theory and Freud in this. For example, in *Eros and Civilization* Marcuse draws on Freud's view that civilization depends upon *repression*. If we tried to gratify all our desires, sexual or otherwise, as and when they occurred, society and civilisation would vanish overnight. Repression is thus inevitable. Marcuse suggests that, in the early stages of capitalism, a high degree of repression is necessary to ensure that people spend most of their energy working and that profits are reinvested rather than enjoyed. Very few desires are allowed into consciousness, and sexual activity is confined to the genitals.

In late capitalist society such a high degree of repression is no longer necessary so that '*surplus repression*' is created. There is more repression than is, in fact, necessary for modern society to remain in existence. This could lead to tension and societal instability. Instead, the capitalist system resists such possible challenges to its control through what Marcuse calls '*repressive desublimation*'. This persuades us to satisfy our desires in ways that are useful to the system. For example, commodities become associated with sex. Naked women are used to sell everything from cars to newspapers. Books and films become more pornographic. All this provides vicarious sexual pleasure. It provides the titillation of sex without actually engaging in it. The sexual desire is satisfied rather than fulfilled.

Frankfurt School theorists thus paint a depressing and pessimistic picture of Western society. It is depressing because mass culture appears to control our internal wishes and desires, as well as our external behaviour through consumption. It is pessimistic because it provides no indication or guidance as to how we might break free of this state of affairs. It is ironic that critical theory, which takes as its starting point the actor's potential to change the world, ends up with an image of that individual as passive, manipulated and dominated.

The structuralist Marxism of Louis Althusser

Structuralist Marxism is often referred to as involving the 'death of the subject'. This is because the theory claims that we are not the authors of our actions. Rather, it is *underlying social structures* which determine how we behave. These structures, which are not obvious, at the surface or visible, work through our activities, and these in turn help either to maintain the structures or, infrequently, change them through revolution. The individual is, therefore, seen as the bearer of invisible structural forms.

The French writer Louis Althusser is one of the best-known structuralist Marxists. Like the Frankfurt School, Althusser argues against the economism of traditional Marxism. But he is also critical of the 'humanism' of the Frankfurt School, regarding it as unscientific. He intends his own Marxism to be a form of science. He claims it is able to produce scientific knowledge about the social world and a political strategy for bringing the working class to power. The means through which this will be achieved is the Communist Party. Although these aims and ambitions may seem fairly straightforward, much of Althusser's writing is complex and difficult. Only a much simplified version can be presented here.

Althusser contends that all societies have three basic levels through which they operate: the economic, the political and the ideological. The political and ideological levels are not simply located in the 'superstructure' and treated as the effects of the economic level, as in other accounts of Marxism. Rather, each level is treated as having *relative autonomy*. By this Althusser means that the political and ideological levels are neither completely dependent on the economic level, nor are they completely independent of it. There is clearly a relationship between the three and, like a good Marxist, Althusser considers economic factors to be very important. But he also acknowledges that the political and ideological levels may, under some circumstances, develop in a fashion which is only partially influenced by the economic. Similarly, he regards it as possible for the political and ideological spheres to act on and effect the economic sphere. Interaction between the three levels is, therefore, conceived to be a complex process. This, he considers, moves his version of Marxism away from crude economic determinism.

Althusser also distances himself from economistic Marxism by arguing that different types of society can be distinguished according to the *dominance* of the different structural levels. So, in the day-to-day development of a society, one particular level can come to be more important than the others. In feudal societies, he regards the political and ideological levels to be predominantly important. Other commentators have, following Althusser, argued that in advanced capitalist society, it is the political which is now dominant. But Althusser himself still claims that it is the structure of the economic level which determines which of the levels is dominant at any particular time. Ian Craib has explained this by suggesting that it is as if the economic level 'hands over' its power to one of the other levels, or keeps it to itself, for the duration of that type of society. Althusser himself describes this in the phrase 'the economic is determinant *in the last instance*'. He therefore argues that, despite the relative autonomy of the political and ideological levels, the economic level does retain some priority in determining how societies become structured and which level will be dominant.

Althusser's theory becomes even more complex when he introduces the concept of '*over-determination*'. Following Marx, he regards capitalist society as being full of inner contradictions, and, for Althusser, these are expressed at the three levels of society. At certain times, he claims, these contradictions are more influential than at others. It is when the contradictions which occur at the various levels come together, to reinforce each other, that capitalism is most vulnerable to revolution, as in the case of the Russian Revolution. On other occasions, the contradictions at one level may be inhibited or negated by factors operating at another level. When this occurs societies drift into stagnation and decay.

Althusser's work has been particularly influential in its emphasis on the state in capitalist society. Whereas Marx seems to argue for the major significance of economic relations, and the Frankfurt School for the importance of mass culture, in the maintenance of the capitalist system, Althusser claims that the state also has a crucial role to play. This is because there are needs to be met which cannot just be fulfilled at the economic level itself. For instance, workers have to be housed, fed and kept in 'good working order'. They need to be educated, both in general and specific skills, and children have to be reared with the right qualities to make them into good workers. Above all, people need to 'know' and be kept in 'their place' so that they do not become discontented, paralysed by hopeless ambition, or threatening to the social order. Such tasks are fulfilled by the state in two ways: firstly, by force – for example, through the army and the police. These are the '*repressive state apparatuses*'. They are used less often than might be the case, however, because of the second means of control. This occurs via the '*ideological state apparatuses*', such as the education system, the media, the family, the Church. By controlling ideas, knowledge and social understanding, these institutions all ensure that people do what the underlying structures demand they do.

Probably the best-known account of an ideological state apparatus is S. Bowles and H. Gintis' *Schooling in Capitalist America* (RKP, 1976). They argue that the education system does not provide equality of opportunity for its students. This is because it mirrors the unequal structure of the capitalist economy and therefore is programmed to produce the kinds of workers with the sorts of skills, views and temperaments that the capitalist system needs. In short, for structuralist Marxists, the structures through which our societal institutions operate work to ensure the maintenance and the continuation of capitalism.

6 Sociological theory and the feminist challenge

Although more than half of the world's population are women, sociology largely ignored them for the first one hundred years or so of its existence. Sociological theory was about men's lives and men's worlds. It was concerned with the alienation which occurred in men's work, with the development of a capitalist system in which class (based upon men's occupations) played a critical part, with evolution and social change where a 'neutered society' became more 'functionally specialised' and 'adaptively upgraded', despite the confinement of many women to the privacy of men's homes.

The late 1960s, however, saw the re-emergence of the women's movement, and sociology as a discipline has been much affected by this. Studies of women's experiences in many areas, ranging from work and the family, health and mental illness, images and the media, to violence and sexuality have been conducted. Women have also pioneered new methods of social enquiry. Here we are not so much concerned with the ways in which feminism has been able to make visible the previously hidden worlds of women. Rather, the focus is on how feminism has begun to challenge and transform the categories and concepts through which sociological theory itself is constructed.

It should be recognised from the start that feminism is not just a perspective which looks at the world from a woman's point of view. It also seeks to understand why women as a group are systematically disadvantaged in most aspects of life. Feminists certainly *describe* the structures through which women's subordination occurs. But they also look for *explanations* as to how the social differences between males and females have arisen, why women face discrimination in a whole range of institutions, and the kind of social changes which would lead to women's greater equality and freedom. Such questions cannot be tackled without a theoretical framework which focuses on the links between different areas of social life and women's position within them. Feminists argue that sociological theories are *gender*-blind because they fail to take account of the differences between men and women and are unable to consider issues relating specifically to women. The commitment of conventional sociology to 'value-neutrality' has resulted in a mask of male political bias. Sociology cannot simply be 'value-free'. The alternative theoretical positions formulated by feminists therefore attempt to unite theory and practice, politics and analysis to promote actively the views and interests of women.

The focus of feminist theory is on women's *oppression*. It is argued that all the disadvantages women encounter – for example, being denied economic, social and political power, suffering violence, sexual assault and harassment – are experienced *because they are women*. The concept of *patriarchy* is used to analyse the principles and structures underlying this oppression. Patriarchy is usually defined as the power relationship by which men dominate women. However, although most feminists are concerned with both oppression and patriarchy, there are differences in the foci and approaches which they have adopted. Most texts divide feminist theory into two kinds: Marxist feminism and radical feminism. This is a useful starting point, but such a simple division tends to overlook some important areas over which there is disagreement. Once these are subjected to scrutiny, it becomes apparent that there are many more kinds of feminism than are usually acknowledged. In fact, rather then femini*sm*, we should probably talk about the existence of femini*sms*. In this respect, the theories which are the focus of this chapter no more comprise a united perspective than any of the others we have previously examined.

The Marxist legacy

Many feminists, particularly in Britain, began their attempt to develop theory by adopting a Marxist framework. This involved seeing gender inequality as rooted within the capitalist economic system. It meant analysing women's oppression in terms which implied that it was a result of capitalism because it was necessary to it. In the early 1970s this form of feminism often took concepts from Marx's work which he had developed to analyse the workplace. It then attempted to make them 'fit' women's experiences in the family and at home.

For instance, the various contributors to what became known as the *Domestic Labour Debate* focused on the issue of the relationship between capitalism and housework. They argued that domestic work should be seen as work in Marx's sense and that it was the basis of women's oppression. Unpaid domestic labour helps to keep down the wages paid by capitalist employers since, if workers had to pay someone to do household servicing for them, a massive increase in wages would be required. Thus, although the housewife appears to work for her own individual family, in reality she works for the maintenance of capitalism. It is this job of doing unpaid domestic service that in the long run benefits capitalism, which constitutes her oppression.

Most feminists, however, object to the simple adoption of Marxist terminology, arguing that ideas developed to explain the conditions of male workers cannot easily be applied to the situation of women. Accordingly, they have tried to alter and extend the Marxist approach, particularly by focusing on the family and women's dependent position within it.

Marxist feminists

Marxist feminists regard the economic position of women as crucial to their oppression. They are particularly interested in the way in which women's position within the family makes them a special target for capitalist exploitation. It is argued that women are given the poorly paid, part-time, low-status jobs because they are regarded as being financially dependent on their husbands, whether or not this is actually the case. This goes unchallenged because everyone – employer, husband and often the wife herself – assumes that a woman's primary role is that of unpaid home-maker. It is the man's job to be the major bread-winner.

Writers such as Veronica Beechey (in *Unequal Work*, Verso, 1987) have explored the implications of this. Beechey argues that married women make useful workers in capitalist societies, since they are relatively cheap to employ. This is because it is not expected that the money they earn has to be sufficient to keep them fully, as the additional wages of the husband do that. Beechey suggests that because of their dependent position in the family and their particularly exploited position in the workforce, married women can be regarded as semi-proletarianised workers.

They are, in fact, economically below the working class.

Other writers, such as Breugal (*Feminist Review*, no. 3, 1979), have argued that married women's economic dependency on their husbands makes them a useful reserve army of labour, which can be moved in and out of the economy as required. Although the effect of this may be tempered – for example, in all-female work-places or in a recession, when keeping on badly-paid women makes economic sense – women's place in the home and their dependency on men means that they can be regarded as marginal workers.

Marxist feminists see women's oppression as having an econ-omic basis which is most clearly reflected in their financial dependence on their husbands. Capitalism has created their dependence to fulfil two functions. Firstly, it provides cheap female workers who can be exploited even more than men. Secondly, it also ensures that household chores are done cheaply. Housewives are not paid for doing these chores because they are treated as services rendered in return for their husbands' provision of relative financial security. Of course, as we have already seen, if wages were paid to housewives this would raise employers' costs. Workers' pay would have to be increased so that they could afford to employ someone to do the housework for them. Such important connections between women's oppression and capi-talism lead Marxist feminists to argue that the interests of women lie with the liberation of the working class and the struggle to overthrow capitalism.

Feminist Marxists

Also working within a broadly Marxist tradition are a group of writers we will call Feminist Marxists. They are critical of the narrow economic focus both of Marx himself and of Marxist feminists. Although agreeing that significance must be given to the role of the capitalist economic system in maintaining women's oppression, they argue that non-economic factors should also be considered. They also stress the importance of the role of ideology in reinforcing women's subordination and male power.

Michele Barrett is an example of one writer who develops this position. In *Women's Oppression Today* (Verso, 1980), she argues that an analysis of ideology, especially that concerning the family, helps to explain why women marry and live in conventional families, when these are the very institutional arrangements which oppress them. Ideology is a powerful factor in encouraging women to accept family life. The nuclear family is presented as natural, inevitable and fulfilling for women. Few positive alternative ways of living are offered to them instead. Barrett is not arguing that the things families have to offer, such as emotional fulfilment, sexual relations and parenthood, are unimportant to human beings. Rather, it is the *ideological assumption* that such needs can and should be fulfilled *only* through a particular type of family system to which she objects. It is this assumption which is oppressive to women. It is uncritical, makes women dependent upon men and automatically sets limits on what women can do and achieve.

Unlike Marxist feminists, feminist Marxists, such as Barrett, do not believe that women's liberation can be achieved solely by overthrowing the economic system of capitalism. Such an economic revolution would be unlikely radically to change other factors, such as the ideological. Changing the economic system is, therefore, only one aspect which is required. Also needed is a change in the relationship between the sexes. For Barrett, women's liberation requires the sharing of tasks such as childcare between men and women, as well as removing women's economic dependence on men. It also necessitates a transformation in the ideology of gender, so that men and women are free to behave as they wish, without having to conform to masculine and feminine stereotypes.

Feminism and Freud

The relationship between oppression and ideology has been explored further by those feminists who are interested in psychoanalysis. In the 1970s, Juliet Mitchell, somewhat controversially, turned to the work of the psychoanalyst Sigmund Freud, whose theories will be examined in the next chapter. She was interested in what Freud had to say that would help us understand how and why women are prepared to accept ideas and institutions which oppress them. She uses Freud's notion of the *unconscious* to argue that ideas about females and femininity have become so taken for granted that we unquestioningly, and often unconsciously, accept them as being natural and inevitable. This means that they are deeply rooted in our personalities and, because of this, very difficult to dislodge or change (*Psychoanalysis and Feminism*, Allen Lane, 1974).

At the time, many feminists were highly critical of Mitchell using Freud's ideas, since his writings about penis envy and female sexuality were widely regarded as sexist. More recently, however, other feminists have seen some usefulness in Freud's work. While theories based upon various forms of Marxism have emphasised the economic and structural aspects of society, psychoanalysis focuses on individuals, their personalities and psyches. This, it is argued, is helpful in understanding both the conscious and unconscious aspects of gender.

An example of this approach is to be found in Nancy Chodorow's book, *The Reproduction of Mothering* (University of California Press, 1978). In her study of mothering and mother-hood, Chodorow wanted to understand why, in a capitalist society, it is assumed that because women give birth to children, they should also bring them up and look after them, often without the help of men. Why do women want and expect to do this? Like most feminists, Chodorow dismisses the idea that mothering is innate. Rather, she focuses on the quality of relation-ships in the family. The relationship between a mother and her daughter is different from that between a mother and her son. Daughters are experienced as extensions of a mother, sons as external and different. Chodorow argues that it is because most women experience intense personal relationships with their mothers, much more so than boys do, that they are able to assume the characteristics and develop the personalities necessary for engaging in mothering behaviour. Women *learn* to be mothers, and they learn the role so intensely that it becomes part and parcel of their self-identity. A woman cannot be forced to take on the behaviour of a mother, says Chodorow, unless she has accepted, at some conscious or unconscious level, that this is part of how she sees herself.

The use of psychoanalytic theory still causes heated debate in feminist circles. However, theorists are increasingly borrowing themes from it to help in the exploration of the psychology of womanhood and femininity.

Materialist feminism

The major exponent of materialist feminism, to date, has been the French feminist Christine Delphy (*Close to Home*, Hutchinson, 1984). Delphy is at pains to distance herself from Marxist feminism. She argues that the essence of Marxism is its *materialist method*, and that Marxists should be wary of simply taking Marx's framework of concepts and applying them uncritically to every situation. Marx's writings were very much a creation of their time, and were designed for a particular purpose. As such, they are not capable of explaining women's oppression. Marx's approach should be adapted if it is to be of use to feminists in the twentieth century. The problem with most feminists who use Marxism is that they give too much attention to a 'genderless proletariat' and not enough to women. Delphy claims to use the *methods of Marxism* rather than its specific content.

Delphy's materialist model involves postulating the existence of two modes of production, the industrial and the domestic. In the industrial mode of production there is capitalist exploitation leading to the formation of two classes, proletariat and bourgeoisie. In the domestic mode of production there is *patriarchal exploitation* and the formation of two classes, men and women. Patriarchal exploitation occurs in the family. It is there that the husband exploits his wife by receiving domestic and sexual services, for which he does not pay. In return for this the husband provides for and keeps his wife. For Delphy, it is this exploitation in the home which enables men to dominate and control women in all other spheres of society. She argues that, from a woman's point of view, *men* and not capitalism are '*the main enemy*' because most women get married and become domestic slaves (see Reading 12).

Delphy also argues that the traditional Marxist view of class, along with various sociological theories, is unable to cope with or account for any of the major aspects of women's oppressed situation. Delphy finds this odd because, after all, the concept 'class' has been a major instrument in developing our understanding of inequality, exploitation and oppression. But, for Delphy, most discussions of class are necessarily about men and not about women. This is because they take the family as the basis for analysis and, usually, equate the socio-economic status of the male head of the household with the class position of the family overall. Delphy argues that this assumes that the family is a harmonious institution, based on equality. It ignores the fact that women are *not* equal to men either in the family or anywhere else. It is the social relationships of power within the family which are the basis through which women are both exploited and oppressed. She therefore holds that men and women, as groups, should be treated as antagonistic and opposing 'classes'. From the materialist feminist viewpoint it is essential that the patriarchal exploitation of women in the home should be looked at, and treated completely separately from, capitalist economic systems.

Capitalism and patriarchy

We have seen that, whereas Marxist feminists hold that the economic system of capitalism is most important in explaining women's oppression, materialist feminists emphasise patriarchy and men's domination and control of women as being most significant. Others have argued that *both* capitalism and patriarchy must be taken into account. There are two versions of this. In the first, exemplified by Zillah Eisenstein, it is argued that women's oppression is the result of patriarchal relations being so intertwined with the relations of capitalism that they form one system (*Capitalist Patriarchy and the Case for Socialist Feminism* (ed.), Monthly Review Press, 1979). This system she calls *capitalist patriarchy*. In it women are oppressed both through the economic system and by men. Capitalism and patriarchy are not two separate and unrelated systems of exploitation. Rather, the two are so mutually dependent that each needs the other in order to survive.

The second version of this thesis is found in the writings of Heidi Hartmann (*The Unhappy Marriage of Marxism and Feminism*, L. Sargent (ed.), Pluto, 1981). She also wishes both capitalism and patriarchy to be taken into account in understanding women's position. But instead of viewing them as one system, she sees them as separate, but coexisting. Capitalism and patriarchy are systems existing autonomously of each other, but they interact and feed into each other at particular points in time. Sometimes they will reinforce each other's structures and assumptions, while at others they will be in contradiction, leading to conflict and tension. This is known as *patriarchal capitalism*.

Radical feminism

The radical feminist position began to develop in the early 1970s. Its impetus came from women who were trying to understand their inferior and secondary role in society and who felt that existing theories, especially those based upon traditional Marxism, did not help in this because of their lack of consideration of women. Radical feminism focuses attention on patriarchy and the role of men in oppressing women. Important in this context was the idea that the *personal is political*. By this was meant that women are not just dominated in the public sphere; they are also oppressed in their private lives and relationships. If politics generally is about power and influencing people, then all relationships are to do with politics. Politics occur in families and between individuals when one person attempts to control or dominate another. It is in the personal and private sphere that women are particularly vulnerable to the power of men. For radical feminists, the most important power relationships are between men and women. This is known as *sexual politics* and refers to the ways in which men individually, and as a group, dominate women and control their lives, particularly in the family and in sexual and personal relations.

Two early radical feminist books, by Shulamith Firestone and Kate Millett, were particularly important in developing non-Marxist feminist theory. In *The Dialectics of Sex*, Firestone focused on male control of women's child-bearing abilities as a source of oppression. Millett, whose book *Sexual Politics* was the first to use that term, examined the ways in which institutions such as the family, the state, ideology and culture continue to produce patriarchy. She argued that this was mainly done through cultural legitimation, acceptance and consent rather than by the use of direct force. In fact, both Millett and Firestone paid only minor attention to violence and sexuality.

Since these books were first published, however, the focus of radical feminism has changed significantly. The active involvement of feminists with women who have been physically and sexually abused means that the analysis of sexuality and violence is now central to radical feminist theory and politics (see Reading 13).

Sexuality

Sexuality refers to those feelings which arouse us and give us pleasure, how we wish to satisfy such feelings and with whom we enjoy fulfilling them. Feminists argue that sexuality is not simply biologically given, but that the form it takes is socially constructed. Indeed, it is constructed by men in a particular kind of way to satisfy their own desires. For instance, women are regarded as sexual objects, penetration is seen as *the* major source of sexual pleasure, and men are expected to take the initiative in relationships. Women, on the other hand, are simply expected to be passive and pretty and be the playthings of men.

Adrienne Rich refers to this as *compulsory heterosexuality* (*Compulsory Heterosexuality and Lesbian Existence*, Only Women Press, 1981). She argues that women are forced into a narrow form of sexual behaviour, from which they themselves derive little erotic pleasure, by men. They are forced into heterosexuality because this is the only socially accepted form of sexuality. Lesbianism is regarded as a deviant or abnormal alternative. Some feminists, however, regard lesbianism as the only means through which women can experience sexual pleasure in a way which is not oppressive. Sexual intercourse with men, they argue, involves women colluding with their main enemy. They also refer to intercourse as man's colonisation of a woman's body. They regard it as an act through which he is able to control her body and ultimately the rest of her life.

Sexuality, male violence and the social control of women

Radical feminists argue that men's role as the initiator in sexual and other relationships has led them to develop aggressive masculine behaviour, which is directed towards women. Men who rape, harass or molest, for example, are not ill or mad. Rather, such acts are simply extensions of behaviour which men consider to be normal and acceptable. If men are encouraged by the media, advertising and widely-used pornography to see women as sexual objects for their pleasure, we cannot be surprised if some men take this to the extreme.

Radical feminists see the social construction of sexuality and male violence against women as inextricably linked. They are oppressive to women in two main ways. Firstly, current views of sexuality denigrate women and encourage men to view them as sexual objects. Secondly, men can and do use violence against women to get their own way in a variety of different situations. However, it is not just violence itself which is oppressive. The fear or threat of violence is sufficient to ensure that women have to modify their behaviour by, for instance, not going out at night for fear of being attacked. In ways such as this, men are able to control women's activities and oppress them.

Radical feminists have focused attention on a number of specific areas in order to explore the links between violence, sexuality and social control. Susan Brownmiller has argued, for example, that rape is significant in men's control of women because it helps all men to keep all women in a state of fear (*Against Our Will*, Penguin, 1976). This is because it is impossible for women to tell which men are safe and which are rapists. Other writers have concentrated upon domestic violence and the widespread use of physical force by men to control their women. Others, such as Andrea Dworkin, have pointed to the fact that pornography lies at the heart of male dominance, since it portrays women as inferior and humiliated beings and distorts the real nature of womanhood (*Pornography*, The Women's Press, 1981).

Thus, radical feminism views men and women as opposing groups, with one controlling the other. The social world is divided by gender into two *separate social 'classes'*. Feminists who follow Marx define 'class' on the basis of the ownership of private property and wealth, so that women and men are to be found amongst both the bourgeoisie and the proletariat. Radical feminists see all women as linked together in the same class position because of their social control and abuse by men. For them, women's liberation is to be achieved by actively challenging the system of patriarchy. However, challenging 'the system' on its own is not enough. Radical feminists argue that change is important for individuals as well as for society overall. Individuals should be encouraged to become aware of women's oppression and to live their lives in a way which is not based on exploitation. We must assume that men will not willingly give up their power over women. Radical feminists therefore emphasise the importance of women forming organisations and groups apart from men. For some these women's groups are simply an addition to their lives with men. Others, known as *separatists*, try to have as little to do with men as possible, and live apart from them.

The black feminist critique of white feminism

The above discussion of feminist theory has emphasised the variety of its approaches. Yet in all its variants it is about *white* feminism: feminism written *by* white women, *about* white women, *for* white women. It has also been mainly produced by *privileged* women – women with educational qualifications, jobs and a reasonable standard of living. That this kind of feminism is partial, exclusive and marginalising has been brought home by black feminists. They have been highly critical of feminism for implying that white experiences are somehow more central and important than those of blacks.

The black feminist critique has been mounted by a wide range of women from different cultures, communities and societies. The term 'black' is not meant to refer to a fixed cultural identity. For example, Afro-Caribbean, Asian and African peoples are included in this rubric. Instead, it is a political category which acknowledges that the political, social and ideological force of racism creates a gulf between white people and those whom they oppress, on both a face-to-face and an institutional basis.

Black feminists have been critical of white feminism in several ways. Firstly, they argue the black women's experiences are simply invisible in it. Feminism has tended to ignore the experiences both of indigenous black women, those living in Britain and the United States, and those who comprise a large proportion of the world's population in the Third World. Secondly, where feminism has bothered to consider black women's experiences, it has treated them as eccentric or bizarre. In Britain this has involved, for instance, a preoccupation with arranged marriages. In other countries it has led to a focus on phenomena such as the veiling of women or female circumcision. This ignores things such as poverty or lack of education with which the women themselves are concerned.

A third criticism of feminist theory has been the implicit racism of its analysis. For example, much of it regards the family as a major site of oppression. Yet for black women the family can be a refuge, a haven in a heartless world of racism, somewhere secure to return from, and develop resistance to, the external world of racism outside. The concept of 'patriarchy' is also a problem since it lumps all men together. But racism ensures that black men do not have the same relationship to capitalist and patriarchal systems as white men. White men and women can and do oppress black men and women.

A fourth criticism relates to the way in which feminists have begun to theorise the interconnection of gender and 'race'. For it tends to be implied that 'race' simply increases the degree of oppression which black women experience as women, and that if this can be 'added in' to our already existing theoretical frameworks, then everything will be all right. But 'race' cannot simply be added on to models which already exist in this way. This is because it does not simply make the experience of women's oppression greater. It qualitatively changes the *nature* of that oppression. Black women are not simply subjected to *more* disadvantage than their white sisters; their oppression, because of racism, is of a qualitatively different kind.

Hence it is no good for white feminists to apologise for not having included black women in their thinking. Black women argue that they often cannot be included because the existing theoretical frameworks have been constructed in such a way that they are not capable of taking account of the experiences which they have as black women. Instead, feminism now has to work towards reconstructing itself in such a way that it can encompass both the complexity and diversity of all women's experiences. Bell Hooks has referred to this as moving from 'margin to centre'. Black women do not wish to be 'tolerated' by white feminists. They want their experiences to be fully reflected in feminist analyses. This does not have to be divisive of feminism. As Hooks says: 'Women do not need to eradicate difference to feel solidarity. We do not need to share common oppressors to fight equally to end oppression (Bell Hooks, *From Margin to Centre*, 1985, South End Press).

7 The illustrious outsiders

So far this book has concentrated on what are usually regarded as the major perspectives in sociological theory. To the conventional list one other has been added, feminism. In the case of each so-called 'perspective', it has been shown that very different approaches are often classified together under the same heading. There is often as much dividing authors who have been placed in a particular category as there is uniting them. A perspectives view of theory, therefore, tends to over-emphasise unity and play down disagreement when looking at particular kinds of sociology.

There is also another way in which the perspectives approach causes difficulties. This is because there are many authors, now and in the past, whose writings simply do not fit into any of the main perspectives categories. Not only does this mean that major intellectual giants are excluded from the perspectives vision of sociology. It also results in the exclusion of some important dimensions of social life from the parameters of theorising.

It is impossible to include in discussion here all those illustrious but 'awkward' writers whose work presents difficulties in terms of classification. Four only have been chosen: Freud, Foucault, Habermas and Giddens. What follows does not comprise, in any sense, an exhaustive account of their ideas. Instead, it is intended to point to some of the most exciting and most fruitful areas which they have tackled.

Sigmund Freud (1865–1939)

Freud was an Austrian who founded the branch of psychology known as psychoanalysis. Psychoanalysis is concerned with understanding the workings of the mind, so it might appear to be a focus of interest which has little relevance to sociology. Freud, however, was concerned with the relationship between the internal functioning of the mind and external factors. He believed that the latter affected the former, with profound consequences for human behaviour. In addition to developing a theory about the operation of the psyche, Freud's pychoanalysis was also a form of therapy. In his clinics Freud tried to treat mental disorders in patients by investigating the interaction between conscious and unconscious elements in the mind, and bringing them into consciousness. He first of all did this through hypnosis, but later changed to the method of 'free association'.

Three major themes emerge from Freud's writing. The first is that of '*repression*' and the '*unconscious*'. Freud believed that a new-born child comprised a bundle of unbridled instincts which needed to be repressed and restrained, if the child was to be properly socialised for life in a civilised society. In the course of learning self-control, primarily taught by parents, a child may go through many difficult experiences. These may be so traumatic that the child represses all aspects of them into the *unconscious* part of the mind. The result is that memories of them are not accessible to conscious thought.

The second theme in Freud's work is his emphasis on the importance of *early childhood experiences*; for the things that are repressed in childhood are the frequent source of problems in adulthood. Hysteria, neurosis, phobias, errors, dreams – even jokes – can all, according to Freud, be traced to repressions early in life. The fears and worries we had then re-emerge in other guises. It takes psychoanalytic therapy to provide the 'cure', by bringing the unconscious memories back into consciousness so that they can be overcome.

The third significant Freudian theme was that of *sexuality*. Freud claimed that many of the repressions which occurred in childhood were sexual. In this he shocked conservative European society with the suggestion that children were sexual beings, with sexual desires. Freud sees the development of heterosexual feelings in men and women as being tied up with the repression and control of these desires in early childhood. Babies are born with a polymorphous sexuality. They have the proclivity to desire either their own or the opposite sex. In learning to channel their sexuality towards the opposite sex, children go through several stages of development, including 'penis envy' and the 'castration complex'. Freud put forward a complex theory as to how girls become feminine and boys masculine, and why their personalities grow to coincide with these gender characteristics. He believed that, to a large extent, this depends on the meaning that children give to genital sex difference, and the relationships which they have with their parents (see Reading 14).

Freud's theories were initially regarded as very controversial. Subsequently, other thinkers revised and developed his ideas. Both Freud and his followers have influenced a wide range of theorists. Of those discussed in this book, for instance, Parsons, Marcuse, Habermas and some forms of feminism have all utilised concepts and analyses drawn from Freud's work. Given this range of influence Freud, although not himself a sociologist, must be regarded as an important figure in the development of the discipline.

Michel Foucault (1926–84)

Foucault, who was French, was particularly influenced intellectually by Marx, Freud and the philosopher Nietzsche. He is usually regarded as a *post-structuralist*, although he himself would have rejected that label as he would also that of 'sociologist'. In 'post-structuralism' we find the idea that the world is created by different kinds of languages, or *discourses*. These construct the world, giving it particular forms.

Foucault's work is primarily concerned with *power*. It reverses the way in which we usually regard the relationship between power and knowledge. Normally we see knowledge as something which gives us power to do things. Without it we would fail or do them badly. However, Foucault argues that knowledge is itself a form of power over others. Knowledge, as constructed in discourse, constitutes *the power to define others*. Knowledge is usually treated as leading to liberation; the more we know, both individually and collectively, the more we 'improve' ourselves and society. Foucault argues that, in fact, knowledge has become a form of enslavement. It is a tool through which particular groups have been isolated, excluded and oppressed.

Foucault's major studies, on madness, medical knowledge, imprisonment and sexuality, all explore this theme in varying ways. For instance, in *Madness and Civilization* (Tavistock, 1977) Foucault claims that all societies need deviants. It is by *excluding* some people, and defining them as having been excluded, that society makes everyone else feel *included*. This is important in maintaining social solidarity. Foucault argues that during the

Middle Ages the necessary deviants in Europe were lepers who were confined in special institutions, excluding them from the rest of the community. However, partly because of this exclusion, leprosy eventually died out. A new sort of deviant therefore had to be created. Eventually the poor, criminals and those with 'deranged minds' were compelled to occupy the space of exclusion which had been vacated by the lepers.

Foucault is particularly interested in those who were eventually locked away because they were considered 'mad'. He notes that, prior to the mid-seventeenth century, madness was regarded as a form of sacred knowledge which could provide insights into the human condition. However, the rise of the notion of rationality and the development of scientific forms of knowledge meant that the idea of madness began to develop a new meaning. Insanity was defined as a particular condition, seen as the opposite of sanity. Such a definition meant that the mad had to be confined. First of all they were put away with the poor and criminals. But, as scientific knowledge developed, the definition of 'madness' came to be refined. It was seen as a disease, which doctors tried to cure through acts of purification, such as making their patients eat soap, tartar or vinegar. Gradually the new discipline of psychiatry began to emerge. This led to different kinds of 'cure' – for instance, leucotomy (making incisions in the brain) and ECT (electroconvulsive therapy: administering controlled shocks).

Foucault argues that the kind of discourse through which different sorts of knowledge about madness has been expressed, historically, has been a discourse about power. It has served to define, explain, cure and structure madness. It has been used *against* those unlucky enough to be regarded as insane, because the insane have been the victims of the kinds of incarceration and treatment which this knowledge advocates.

Foucault regards all forms of discourse as having rules as to who can make statements and when they can be made. These, of course, necessarily include some people and exclude others. He sees the world as comprising a myriad of power relations, each based on different forms of knowledge. Individuals are placed among these different kinds of discourse, which are structured independently of them and are outside of their control. They are constantly being pushed around by them. But at the same time, says Foucault, people are always *striving* to get some control of discourses – and their lives. In this sense movements of resistance can develop. His position is, therefore, one which attempts to acknowledge the existence of both a determining structure and acting, struggling individuals. It is a theory which has been very important in stressing the relationship between discourse, knowledge and power.

Jurgen Habermas (1929–   )

The German theorist, Habermas, was a student of those involved in the Frankfurt School of critical theory, and he is usually regarded as extending their work. An important starting point in getting to grips with his theory is the distinction he makes between three types of knowledge, which he sees as governed by particular kinds of 'interests'.

Firstly, there is the *'technical interest'*, which wants to master and control natural processes and use them to our advantage. This leads to what Habermas calls *'the empirico-analytic sciences'*, or positivism. Secondly, there is the *'practical interest'*. This is concerned with human interaction and interpretation, the way we understand each other and act collectively. This leads to *'historical-hermeneutic sciences'*; symbolic interaction and ethnomethodology could be regarded as being of this kind. Thirdly, there is the *'emancipatory interest'*. This gives rise to the *'critical social sciences'* which are rooted in our ability to think, reflect and change our circumstances. Habermas takes psychoanalysis as the model of a critical social science because this clearly attempts to reveal to a patient the unconscious processes which determine action and bring them under conscious control. It is the kind of theory he hopes he himself is developing.

Habermas is critical of the way in which the positivistic sciences dominate, and have increasingly gained priority over other forms of knowledge. Since the late nineteenth century there has been a growing interdependence of science, technology and production. In fact, according to Habermas, science and technology have become a leading productive force in society. The economy appears to depend on the process of technical innovation. The problems facing capitalist economies are defined as technical, to be dealt with by experts. As a consequence, politics has become 'negative' in character. It is concerned with maintaining the system and making adjustments so that it runs in a technically efficient way, rather than offering a fundamental political critique of it.

Although the basic concepts of Habermas's framework are derived from Marx, he does point to two new developments which are significant. The first is the transformation of science and technology into a leading productive force, so that they can no longer be regarded as simply 'ideology' and part of the superstructure. The second concerns the growing role of the state. This Habermas regards as particularly dangerous, since the state now regulates not only the economy but almost every area of public life. It does this in a scientistic and technocratic fashion, which again emphasises efficiency and control rather than reflection and critique. All this suggests that Marx's original model requires some reformulation.

Habermas does this by developing a theory of social evolution, which many of his critics have likened to that developed by Talcott Parsons. This is also why his work is not easily bracketed as merely an extension of the Frankfurt School's. In this theory Habermas claims that the economic level of society is only dominant in early capitalism, rather than forming the basis of *all* social systems. Instead, each different kind of society is governed by a particular institutional complex which is specific to it. For example, it might be economic institutions for early capitalism, the state in late capitalism and the kinship system in tribal societies. Each set of institutions embody certain cultural norms and values. These progress to higher levels of generality and universality as societies develop and evolve. They also entail decreasing amounts of repression, since societies come to be increasingly integrated through shared cultural values. All this, of course, sounds very much like Parsons.

This model of social evolution forms the backcloth for Habermas's *analysis of crises* in advanced capitalism. He identifies four types of crisis (reminiscent this time of Parsons' functional imperatives!). Each stage of capitalism's development leads to a new type, although the previous one may not necessarily have been solved or eliminated. In early capitalism *economic crises* are most important. Increasing state intervention leads to a *rationality crisis*. This is rooted in the inability of the state to build an orderly society out of the conflicting interests of private capital. Then a *legitimacy crisis* develops, because if the state cannot produce order it loses its legitimacy to rule in the eyes of the population. The justification for its existence falters. This brings about the fourth crisis, a *motivational crisis*. All the other crises undermine people's motivation for participating in the system at all. There seems little point in working, voting, or any other similar sort of activity. Habermas contends that capitalist societies have reached the stage of legitimation crisis. If the motivation crisis also occurs there is the possibility of transforming the social system into one based on socialist principles.

Anthony Giddens

Giddens is the most prominent British sociologist of our time. He is a prolific writer, drawing on a wide variety of thinkers – Marx, Weber, Mead, Schutz and Foucault, for instance. Much of his early work involved a review of the thinking of these scholars in an attempt to synthesise from them what he considered to be the most important elements for the construction of sociological theory. A reappraisal of Marxism, for instance, suggested that it was too economistic and denied the role of human agency in maintaining and changing the social order. This suggested to Giddens that we need to conceptualise 'structural constraint' in a new way.

Giddens does this through his *theory of structuration*. This is an ambitious attempt to bring about a synthesis of different and often opposed intellectual traditions. He points to what he calls the *'dualism of agency and structure'*. A number of different kinds of thinkers have elaborated highly sophisticated accounts of human conduct, incorporating the actor's meanings, beliefs, desires and intentions. But they have paid little attention to the structural features of society. Similarly, those writers who have focused on structures have ignored the place of individual actors in their theories. Giddens' aim is to overcome this separation of agency and structure. He seeks to retain the stress on meaning offered by interpretive sociologists, while also acknowledging the importance, asserted by Parsons and Marxists alike, of social structures in shaping human conduct.

Giddens' *theory of structuration* starts from the assumption that society is produced or 'made to happen' by human beings through their actions. But this does not occur in circumstances of an individual's own choosing. We are born into a world which is already formed, patterned and organised. Our actions are there-fore guided by this pre-given form.

Giddens distinguishes between *social structures* and *social systems* (as indeed does Parsons). Social structures comprise the un-intended consequences of human conduct, which set the bound-aries for how it is possible for individuals to act. Social systems are human collectivities which persist over time. The persistence of a social system is due to the kind of structures which are embedded in it. Giddens distinguishes between three different dimensions of structure. *Signification* is where agents rationalise or make their actions conform through communication, interpret-ation and interaction. *Domination* is where there is asymmetry or inequality in the distribution of available resources. *Legitimation* is where different forms of conduct are sanctioned through shared norms.

Two other guiding tenets of Giddens' work are distinctively anti-functionalist in nature. The first exhorts the sociologist not to look for the functions of social phenomena but for the *contra-dictions* they involve. The implication of this is contained within his second principle. This conceptualises structures as enabling, as well as constraining, individual action. They do not simply limit the scope of human conduct, but also make certain kinds of activity possible. Giddens claims that, although structures shape the actions of individuals, it is only through these activities that the structures themselves have any effect. In fact, they may them-selves be modified by individual action. He refers to this as the '*duality of structure*'. In this way his theory brings together the (hitherto) largely separated notions of structure and action.

In his recent writings Giddens has laid out what he regards as the main elements for sociological theory in the future (see Reading 15). He argues that much contemporary theory is far too concerned with issues derived from nineteenth-century thinking which are today redundant. Instead, sociology should focus on issues such as rapid technological change, the proliferation of nuclear weapons, conditions of living in the Third World, mili-tary power and war. He believes that a *world system* has developed in the twentieth century, which should also be the focus of analysis. The increasing interconnectedness of the modern world means that it no longer makes sense to concentrate on individual societies. Instead, sociology should emphasise the problems of global society and how these should be resolved.

Giddens' image of sociology's future and the prospect for sociological theory

Giddens argues that sociology's fitness for such an ambitious future project will depend on its making three particular changes. It must turn its back on the dead thinkers of the last century and develop new concepts and frameworks suitable for dealing with the transformed society in which we now live. Secondly, sociology should try to break down the divisions between itself and other social sciences, so that the insights of politics, economics and social policy can be properly used. Thirdly, the barriers within sociology itself should be tackled by challenging the divisions between theory and methods; abstract theorising and empirical projects; 'academic' sociology and its involvement in, and commitment to, issues in the 'real' world. Giddens' view is that this will involve reconciliation and synthesis.

All this will probably also involve sociology abandoning the 'perspectives' approach and replacing it with an emphasis on theorising as a process. Indeed, Giddens himself has concluded that 'The time when it seemed that the advocates of the competing theoretical schools simply inhabited different universes, hermetically sealed off from one another, is now surely past'. The sociological tradition has always involved not just a commitment to the intellectual values of the discipline, but a practical and political involvement in society. If this is to be maintained, then sociology can ill afford for its theorising to consist of cerebral gymnastics alone. If it is to remain active in the modern world, sociology may have to recapture the pragmatism which has served many of its leading exponents well, and which was advocated in the opening chapter of this book.

PART 3

Documentary readings

8 Documentary readings

Reading 1 The rules of sociological method

In *The Rules of Sociological Method*, Durkheim sets out to describe the science of society. In the following extract the main elements of this are outlined.

Durkheim's aim is to demonstrate that there may and must be a sociology which is an objective science conforming to the model of the other sciences, and whose subject is the social fact. First, the subject of this science must be specific, it must be distinguished from the subjects of all the other sciences. Second, this subject must be such as to be observed and explained in a manner similar to the way in which facts are observed and explained in the other sciences.

This twofold requirement leads to the two celebrated formulas. . . . First, social facts must be regarded as things: and second, the characteristic of the social fact is that it exercises a constraint on individuals. . . .

Durkheim's point of departure is that we do not know, in the scientific sense of the word *know*, what the social phenomena which surround us, among which we live, . . . really are. . . . This does not mean that we do not have some idea of them; but precisely because we have a vague and confused idea of them, it is important to regard social facts as things, i.e. to rid ourselves of the preconceptions and prejudices which incapacitate us when we try to know social facts scientifically. We must observe social facts from the outside; we must discover them as we discover physical facts. . . .

How do we recognise a social phenomenon? We recognise

it by the fact that it forces itself on the individual. And Durkheim gives a series of extremely varied examples which show the multiplicity of meanings with which the term *constraint* is invested in his thinking. There is constraint when, in a gathering or a crowd, a feeling imposes itself on everyone, or a collective reaction – laughter, for example – is communicated to all. Such a phenomenon is typically social in Durkheim's eyes because its basis, its subject, is the group as a whole and not one individual in particular. Similarly, there is a social phenomenon in the case of fashion; everyone dresses in a certain way in a given year because everyone else does so. It is not an individual which is the cause of fashion, it is society itself which expresses itself in these implicit and diffuse obligations.

(Raymond Aron, *Main Currents in Sociological Thought*, vol. 2, Weidenfeld and Nicolson, 1968)

Questions

1 Describe five examples in social life where social constraint, in the sense meant by Durkheim, clearly dictates the behaviour of the individual.
2 Is it possible to explain soccer hooliganism or rioting with reference to Durkheim's *Rules* alone?
3 Why might Durkheim's *Rules* be regarded as an example of positivism?

Reading 2 Suicide

There have been many criticisms of Durkheim's study of *Suicide*. In the extract below the views of a recent critic, Jack Douglas, are outlined.

Durkheim was interested in locating the social causes of a certain form of behaviour: suicide. Having given his own definition of suicide, he used the official statistics as the operational measure of the 'real' rate of suicide as he had defined it. Douglas argues that if we look at the workings of the official agencies, it will be seen that in each and every case of a death being investigated, officials are involved in interpreting the world, of deciding that this is, or is not, a suitable motive for suicide; that this cannot be a suicide because nobody would

intentionally kill themselves in that way for that reason. . . .
What ends up in the official statistics as a suicide can be the
outcome of a lengthy process of decision-making, involving
in any one case the assignment of particular social meanings
to social events. Durkheim assumed that a suicide was an easy
thing to see and that the social meaning of suicide was unprob-
lematic. For him, there are out in the world certain objects
describable as suicides; for Douglas, this uncritical acceptance
of the official statistics as unproblematic represents the positivist approach at its crudest.

By contrast, Douglas suggests that we look at detailed case
studies of deaths defined as suicide. By examining the construction of meaning in particular contexts, we will eventually be
able to classify different patterns of suicidal meanings. The
message is clear: suicide is a matter of social definition and
these definitions vary; there is nothing 'out there' with the
intrinsic meaning 'suicide'. The way forward is to analyse the
meanings our subjects attach to the world. To do so, we must
look in depth at their words and actions in all their qualitative
detail.

(E. C. Cuff and G. C. F. Payne, *Perspectives in Sociology*,
1984)

Questions

1 What is the implication of Douglas' position for the sociological study of deviancy and education?
2 Is the implication of Douglas' critique of Durkheim that there
is nothing 'really real' about the social world, such as poverty
or unemployment?

Reading 3   A functionalist analysis of prostitution

The following reading is taken from a theorist, Kingsley Davis,
who is regarded as having been a leading exponent of functionalism. Here he analyses prostitution in functionalist terms.

We can imagine a social system in which the motive for prostitution would be completely absent, but we cannot imagine
that the system would ever come to pass. It would be a regime
of absolute sexual freedom, wherein intercourse were practiced

solely for the pleasure of it, by both parties. This would entail at least two conditions: *First*, there could be no institutional control of sexual expression. Marriage, with its concomitants of engagement, jealousy, divorce, and legitimacy, could not exist. Such an institution builds upon and limits the sexual urge, making sex expression contingent upon non-sexual factors, and thereby paving the way for intercourse against one's physical inclinations. *Second*, all sexual desire would have to be mutually complementary. One person could not be erotically attracted to a non-responsive person, because such a situation would inevitably involve frustration and give a motive for using force, fraud, authority, or money to induce the unwilling person to co-operate.

Neither of these conditions can in the nature of things come to pass. As we have seen, every society attempts to control, and for its own survival must control, the sexual impulse in the interests of social order, procreation, and socialisation. Moreover, all men are not born handsome nor all women beautiful. Instead there is a perfect gradation from extremely attractive to extremely unattractive, with an unfavourable balance of the old and ugly. This being the case, the persons at the wrong end of the scale must, and inevitably will, use extraneous means to obtain gratification. . . .

Not only will there always be a set of reproductive institutions which place a check upon sexual liberty, a system of social dominance which gives a motive for selling sexual favours, and a scale of attractiveness which creates the need for buying these favours, but prostitution is, in the last analysis, economical. Enabling a small number of women to take care of a large number of men, it is the most convenient sexual outlet for an army, and for the legions of strangers, perverts, and physically repulsive in our midst. It performs a function, apparently, which no other institution fully performs.

(Kingsley Davis, 'The Sociology of Prostitution', *American Sociological Review*, vol. 2, 1937)

Questions

1 Make a list of the beliefs and values which seem to underlie this objective scientific analysis.

2   What functions does prostitution fulfil, according to Davis,
and who seems to benefit from it?
3   Does this account help us to understand the persistence of
prostitution and why women become prostitutes?

Reading 4   Parsons' pattern variables

In Chapter 3, mention was made of the 'pattern variables' as being
important in the early stages of Parsons' work. A pattern variable
is a set of two mutually exclusive kinds of *choice* that may face
any given individual prior to action. Below, the details of these
'choices' are presented more fully.

1   *Affectivity or affective neutrality*: whether emotional involvement
and personal feeling is appropriate (e.g., in a family) or should
be suppressed (e.g. in medical practice).

2   *Specificity or diffuseness*: whether the action is specific and
narrowly defined to a particular relationship (e.g. a specific
commercial transaction in a shop) or whether the relationship
is multi-faceted (e.g. parent and child).

3   *Universalism or particularism*: whether participants in an interaction should be treated according to some objective and
universalistic standard (e.g. all equal before the law), or
whether account should be taken of a particular feature of the
relationship (e.g. loyalty to one's friend).

4   *Achievement or ascription*: whether emphasis should be given to
what someone or something can do (e.g. choosing the best
person for the job), or to some attribute (e.g. sex, age, race
or family status).

5   *Self or collectivity*; whether an action should be pursued in
private self-interest, or whether it should be undertaken in the
interests of some wider group or collective interest.

(This last pattern variable was left out of Parsons' later
formulations.)

Questions

1   How would these pattern variables apply to your choice of

action when relating to a supermarket checkout operator, your boyfriend/girlfriend, a teacher and a parent?

2 Are these pattern variable 'choices' in fact dichotomous and mutually exclusive?

Reading 5 *Phenomenology in the classroom*

Phenomenological theory has had one of its major impacts on the sociology of education. In the following, the work of one influential writer in this area is discussed:

> (Nell Keddie) . . . argues that many of the proposed remedies for the educational failure of the working–class child . . . will be ineffective if 'hierarchical categories of ability and knowledge' persist. In other words, it is the teacher's notions of 'high and low ability' and their view of the nature of knowledge which are at fault. . . .
>
> Keddie points out that, at the school she studied, ability is conceptualised in terms of whether or not pupils can manage material or knowledge appropriate to a particular ability band. According to the teachers, A–stream pupils have the ability to 'master subjects'. They can cope with the abstract, intellectual material. C–stream pupils, on the other hand, need more concrete, familiar, illustrative material which is rooted in experience and couched in a language they can understand. Basically they are unable to master subjects and require material which is, so to speak, 'nearer home'.
>
> Keddie's own interpretation of events is rather different from that of the teachers. We should not, she believes, see the differences between A– and C–stream pupils in terms of the one being superior to the other; rather, they have contrasting approaches to knowledge. Of the A–stream pupil's supposed ability to master subjects, she says:
>
> 'This is not necessarily a question of the ability to move to higher levels of generalisation and abstraction so much as an ability to move into an alternative system of thought from that of his everyday knowledge. In practical terms this means being able to work within the framework which the teacher constructs and by which the teacher is then himself constrained.'

. . . C-stream pupils, on the other hand, do not operate within the confines of a subject in this way and are primarily concerned with the everyday meaning of an issue. They are also more likely to question the value of what they are taught as opposed to only raising questions within the framework of the subject. Consequently, the teacher defines such pupils as unable to master subjects and adjusts her expectations of them accordingly. But such expectations have a major impact on educational achievement, stresses Keddie. As she says: 'It seems likely that it is here that teachers' expectations of pupils most effectively operate to set levels of pupil achievement'. In other words, the teachers create failure.

(D. Blackledge and B. Hunt, *Sociological Interpretations of Education*, Croom Helm, 1985)

Questions

1 Why should Keddie's work be regarded as 'interpretive' sociology?
2 Phenomenologists argue that actors have to create 'typifications' in the process of giving meaning to everyday life. In your own observations of teacher–pupil interactions, what kinds of 'typifications' do you think teachers use and how do they arrive at them?

Reading 6   *The ethnomethodology of gender*

Our purpose in this article is to propose an ethnomethodologically informed, and therefore distinctively sociological, understanding of gender as a routine, methodical, and recurring accomplishment. We contend that the 'doing' of gender is undertaken by women and men whose competence as members of society is hostage to its production. Doing gender involves a complex of socially guided perceptual, interactional, and micropolitical activities that cast particular pursuits as expressions of masculine and feminine 'natures'. . . .

Garfinkel's case study of Agnes, a transsexual raised as a boy who adopted a female identity at aged 17 and underwent a sex reassignment operation several years later, demonstrates how gender is created through interaction and at the same time structures interaction. Agnes, whom Garfinkel characterised as a 'practical methodologist', developed a number of procedures for passing as a 'normal, natural female' both prior to and after her surgery. She had the practical task of managing the fact that she possessed male genitalia and that she lacked the social resources a girl's biography would presumably provide in everyday interaction. In short, she needed to display herself as a woman, simultaneously learning what it was to be a woman. . . . Agnes had to consciously contrive what the vast majority of women do without thinking. She was not 'faking' what 'real' women do naturally. She was obliged to analyse and figure out how to act within socially structured circumstances and conceptions of femininity that women born with appropriate biological credentials come to take for granted early on. As in the case of others who must 'pass', such as transvestites, . . . or Dustin Hoffman's 'Tootsie', Agnes's case makes visible what culture has made invisible – the accomplishment of gender.

(C. West and D. H. Zimmerman 'Doing Gender', *Gender and Society*, vol. 1., no. 2, June 1987)

Questions

1 Try to imagine that you have to 'pass' as a member of the opposite sex. What taken-for-granted, everyday aspects of gender temperament and behaviour would be revealed?
2 Why does Garfinkel refer to Agnes as a 'practical methodologist'?

Reading 7 Symbolic interactionism, learning and deviancy

In his account of marihuana (cannabis) use, Becker describes the ways in which experiences are defined and interpreted through learning and interaction.

. . . The novice does not normally get high the first time he smokes marihuana, and several attempts are usually necessary to induce this state. One explanation of this may be that the drug is not smoked 'properly', that is, in a way that insures sufficient dosage to produce real symptoms of intoxication. . . .

The first step in the sequence of events that must occur if the person is to become a user is that he must learn to use the proper smoking technique in order that his use of the drug will produce some effects in terms of which his conception of it can change.

Such a change is, as might be expected, a result of the individual's participation in groups in which marihuana is used. In them the individual learns the proper way to smoke the drug. . . .

Even after he learns the proper smoking technique, the new user may not get high and thus not form a conception of the drug as something which can be used for pleasure. . . . It is not enough, that is, that the effects be present; they alone do not automatically provide the experience of being high. The user must be able to point them out to himself and consciously connect them with his having smoked marihuana before he can have this experience. Otherwise, regardless of the actual effects produced, he considers that the drug has had no effect on him. . . . It is only when the novice becomes able to get high in this sense that he will continue to use marihuana for pleasure. . . .

One more step is necessary if the user who has now learned to get high is to continue use. He must learn to enjoy the effects he has just learned to experience. Marihuana–produced sensations are not automatically or necessarily pleasurable. . . . The user feels dizzy, thirsty; his scalp tingles; he misjudges time and distances; and so on. Are these things pleasurable? He isn't sure. If he is to continue marihuana use, he must decide that they are. Otherwise, getting high, while a real enough experience, will be an unpleasant one he would rather avoid. . . . In summary, an individual will be able to use marihuana for pleasure only when he goes through a process of learning to conceive of it as an object which can be used in this way. . . . [Thus] The presence of a given kind of behaviour is the result of a sequence of social experiences during which the person acquires a conception of the meaning of the behaviour, and perceptions and judgments of objects and situations, all of which make the activity possible and desirable. Thus, the motivation or disposition to engage in the activity is built up in the course of learning to engage in it and does not antedate this learning process.

(H. S. Becker, 'Becoming a Marihuana User', *The American Journal of Sociology*, Nov. 1953)

Questions

1 What are the main elements of Becker's theoretical approach?
2 How might this be usefully applied to situations of interest to sociologists of education and deviancy?

Reading 8 *Marx's materialist model of society*

In the following extract Marx is regarded as having made his most succinct statement about the materialist approach to analysing society.

> In the social production of their life, men enter into definite relations that are indispensable and independent of their will, relations of production which correspond to a definite stage of development of their material productive forces. The sum total of these relations of production constitutes the economic structure of society, the real foundation, on which rises a legal and political superstructure and to which correspond definite forms of social consciousness. The mode of production of material life conditions the social, political and intellectual life process in general. It is not the consciousness of men that determines their being, but on the contrary, their social being that determines their consciousness. At a certain stage of their development, the material productive forces of society come in conflict with the existing relations of production, or – what is but a legal expression for the same thing – with the property relations within which they have been at work hitherto. From forms of development of the productive forces these relations turn into their fetters. Then begins an epoch of social revolution. With the change of the economic foundation the entire immense superstructure is more or less rapidly transformed.
>
> (K. Marx, 'Preface to a Contribution to the Critique of Political Economy', in K. Marx and F. Engels, *Selected Works*, Lawrence and Wishart, 1968)

Questions

1 What does Marx mean by 'social being', and why does he think it is so important?
2 Why should the transformation of the superstructure follow on from changes in the economic structure?

Reading 9   Different categories of class

In this extract, Anthony Giddens suggests that there is more to Marx's theory of class than the simple bi-polar model with which he is usually associated.

While . . . [Marx's] . . . dichotomous division is the main 'axis' of the social structure, this simple class relation is complicated by the existence of three other sorts of grouping, two of which are 'classes' in a straightforward sense, while the third is a marginal case in this respect. These are: (1) 'Transitional classes' which are in the process of formation within a society based upon a class system which is becoming 'obsolete': this is the case with the rise of the bourgeoisie and 'free' urban proletariat within feudalism. (2) 'Transitional classes' which, on the contrary, represent elements of a superseded set of relations of production that linger on within a new form of society – as is found in the capitalist societies of nineteenth-century Europe, where the 'feudal classes' remain of definite significance within the social structure. Each of the first two examples results from the application of two dichotomous schemes to a single form of historical society. They represent, as it were, the fact that radical social change is not accomplished over night, but constitutes an extended process of development, such that there is a massive overlap between types of dichotomous class system. (3) The third category includes two principal historical examples: the slaves of the Ancient world, and the independent peasantry of the medieval and post-medieval period. These are 'quasi-class groupings', in the sense that they may be said to share certain common economic interests; but each of them, for different reasons, stands on the margin of the dominant set of class relationships within the societies of which they form part. To these three categories, we may add a fourth 'complicating factor' of the abstract dichotomous system. (4) Sectors or subdivisions of classes. Classes are not homogeneous entities as regards the social relations to which they give rise: Marx recognises various sorts of differentiations within classes.

It should be noted that none of these categories involves sacrificing the abstract conception of the dichotomous class system: but they do make possible the recognition of the existence of 'middle classes', which in some sense intervene between

the dominant and subordinate class. 'Middle classes' are either of a transitional type, or they are segments of the major classes.
(A. Giddens, *The Class Structure of the Advanced Societies*, Hutchinson, 1973)

Questions

1 How would this account of Marx's work help us to understand the role of the aristocracy in Britain today? How would Marx categorise such people?
2 Where would such groups as the unemployed, women and black workers in South Africa figure in such an analysis?

Reading 10   Tensions and contradictions within the capitalist system

In Chapter 5 we saw that Marx believed that the capitalist system comprised tensions and contradictions which would ultimately lead to its demise. Below, Raymond Aron describes the nature of two of these: proletarianisation and pauperisation.

Proletarianisation means that, along with the development of the capitalist regime, the intermediate strata between capitalist and proletarians will be worn thin and that an increasing number of the representatives of these intermediate strata will be absorbed by the proletariat. Pauperisation is the process by which the proletarians tend to grow poorer and poorer as the forces of production are developed. If we assume that, as more is produced, the purchasing power of the working masses is increasingly limited, it is indeed probable that the masses will have a tendency to rebel. According to this hypothesis, the mechanism of the self-destruction of capitalism is a sociological one and operates through the behaviour of social groups.

There is also an alternative Marxist hypothesis: The income distributed to the masses is inadequate to absorb the increasing production, and there results a paralysis of the system, for the latter would be incapable of establishing an equilibrium between the commodities produced and the commodities demanded on the market by consumers.

There are, then, two possible representations of . . . capitalist . . . self-destruction: . . . economic . . . which is a new version of the contradiction between the constantly increasing forces of production and the relations of production that determine the income distributed to the masses, and . . . sociological . . . via the growing dissatisfaction and revolt of the proletarianised workers.

(Raymond Aron, *Main Currents in Sociological Thought*, vol. 1, Penguin, 1968)

Question

1 Are the proletarianisation and pauperisation described above actually occurring? If yes, describe the contemporary mechanisms through which this is taking place. If no, what factors are inhibiting their development?

Reading 11   Critical theory's criticism of positivism

The Frankfurt School of critical theory developed a sustained critique of positivistic sociology. The main elements of this are briefly outlined below.

1 Positivism focuses on *specific* social issues rather than the complex totality of society.

2 Positivism implies that problems can be solved by reforming parts of society, rather than seeing them as being created by the way society as a whole is structured.

3 Positivism focuses only on things that can be observed and are therefore 'on the surface', rather than things which are hidden or the underlying links between them.

4 Positivism's defence of scientific objectivity and value-neutrality is itself a value-commitment – one which supports the status quo.

5 Positivism is unable to be critical of society.

6 Positivism is unable to conceive of the possibility of things being otherwise than they are.

Questions

1 Choose a piece of empirical sociological research with which

you are familiar and which you regard as 'positivistic'. Do any
of the above criticisms apply to it?
2 Choose another piece of empirical research which you think
   would normally be considered as 'interpretive' sociology.
   Apply the above criticisms to this work.

Reading 12   Materialist feminism: men as the main enemy

Patriarchal exploitation is the common, specific and main
oppression of women;

1 *Common*: because it affects all married women;

2 *Specific*: because only women are under an obligation to
   perform free domestic services;

3 *Main*: because even when women go out to work, the class
   membership they derive from that work is conditioned by
   their exploitation as women in the following ways. First,
   because access to the means of production was forbidden
   them by marriage laws . . . and by the practice of inherit-
   ance. . . . Second, because their earnings are cancelled out
   by the deduction of the value of the services which they are
   obliged to buy to replace their own unpaid services. And
   third, because the material conditions for the exercise of
   their outside occupation are dictated by patriarchal oppression. On the one hand, the very possibility of women
   being employed is conditional on their fulfilling their
   primary 'family duties', which results in the work they do
   outside the home being either impossible or else added to
   their domestic work; while on the other, family duties are
   erected as a handicap by capitalism and used as a pretext
   to exploit women in their outside work.

   . . . The control of reproduction is both the cause and the
means for the second great material oppression of women –
sexual exploitation. Control of reproduction is the second facet
of the oppression of women. Establishing why and how these
two forms of exploitation are affected and reinforced by each
other, and why and how both have the same framework and
institution, the family, should be one of the primary theoretical
goals.

   (C. Delphy, *Close to Home*, Hutchinson, 1984)

Questions

1 What does this extract tell us about the main characteristics of patriarchy, as seen by Delphy?
2 How far does Delphy's model help us to understand the position of women in contemporary Britain?

Reading 13   *Violence against women*

Women's experience of sexual and/or physical intimidation and violence – much of it the result of what is assumed to be typical male behaviour – is an integral part of women's lives. It is so common women would like to take it for granted: instead, we take our fear for granted. Women know about the unpredictability of men's physical and sexual intimidation. We plan our lives around it: finding the right street to walk down when coming home, cooking the eggs the way the husband likes them, and avoiding office parties are examples of strategies designed to avoid male sexual and physical intimidation and violence. None of them are foolproof.

Women's engendered vulnerability to intimidating and violent male behaviour is due to their social position, not their biological position. That physical and/or sexual intrusion can happen, with little or no interference from others (and even, to some extent, encouragement) is a declaration of women's powerlessness.

The physical and/or sexual abuse of women is a manifestation of male domination itself; so often characterised as typical, it has been seen to be a natural right of men. According to women's experiences, much of male sexual and physical aggression toward them is not prohibited; it is regulated. Fathers have the right to use their daughters as they please; husbands, their wives; bosses, their female employees; even men unknown to us act as if they have the right to comment on or abuse any woman's body. The fact that all men do not exercise this right is irrelevant to the power afforded to men *as a gender* over women *as a gender*.

(Elizabeth A. Stanko, *Intimate Intrusions*, RKP, 1985)

Questions

1 Stanko claims that *all* women live in fear of male intimidation

and violence, and that this is the basis of their oppression. Do you agree?

2 Many radical feminists claim that because *all* women fear violence, this gives them a common interest making them into a 'class' based on gender. Can women be termed a 'class' on this basis?

Reading 14 *Freud and sexuality*

The following extract outlines Freud's views on childhood sexuality and the importance of parents in its development.

Freud implies that the first discovery by the child of the genital sex difference is always accompanied by preference for the penis. . . . As children come to recognise that girls indeed do not have penises they suppose, says Freud, that this is the result of castration: boys assume that the girl had a penis initially but has since been castrated, while the girl supposes that she has been castrated and that her lack of a penis is the result of 'a punishment personal to herself'.

. . . Phallic eroticism leads the boy to entertain phallic . . . desires in relation to his primary love-object, his mother. This brings him into direct rivalry with his father: that is, it launches him into the Oedipus complex. His belief that girls have been castrated, together with the fact that he has himself already been threatened, either explicitly or implicitly, with castration, leads the boy to fear that his father will retaliate against his phallic desire for his mother by castrating him. He therefore abandons his Oedipus complex and replaces his attachment to his mother by identification with his father. The boy thus comes to embark on his specifically masculine destiny.

For the girl, the dawning of phallic eroticism leads, in Freud's view, to envy of the boy's penis. . . . the girl discovers at some point that her lack of a penis is not specific to herself but is universal in women, that she has not been castrated but was born without a penis. This discovery, involving as it does the recognition that her mother also lacks a penis, leads her to change her attitude to her mother: the mother now 'suffers a great depreciation' in her daughter's eyes. . . . It is these developments, he says, which lead the girl to abandon her mother as primary love-object. She now loosens her attachment to her mother and turns to her father. . . . In sum, penis envy and its resolution are responsible, in Freud's view, for launching the girl on the path towards her feminine destiny.

(J. Sayers, *Biological Politics*, Tavistock, 1982)

Questions

1   Freud's view of childhood is one which sees it as crucial for the development of heterosexuality. Describe the processes through which this occurs.
2   Some feminists have claimed that Freud's views are sexist. On what grounds might such claims be made? Are they justified?

Reading 15   The new rules of sociological method

Giddens' critique of classical sociological theory led him to produce some basic rules about the constituent elements involved in 'adequate' theorising. This was done in deliberate counterpoint to the *Rules* written by Durkheim in the nineteenth century. For Giddens, the primary tasks for sociological analysis are the understanding of actors' meanings, as well as the analysis of social structures and how they are maintained and reproduced.

A. ONE: Sociology is not concerned with a 'pre-given' universe of objects, but with one which is constituted or produced by the active doings of subjects.

TWO: The production and reproduction of society . . . has to be treated as a skilled performance on the part of its members, not as merely a mechanical series of processes.

B. ONE: The realm of human agency is bounded. Men produce society, but they do so as historically located actors, and not under conditions of their own choosing.

TWO: Structures must not be conceptualised as simply placing constraints upon human agency, but as enabling. This is what I call the duality of structure. [Giddens uses the term 'structuration' to refer to the fact that structures are produced by action but that actions also take place in the context of them.]

THREE: Processes of structuration involve an interplay of meanings, norms and power.

C. ONE: The sociological observer cannot make social life available as a 'phenomenon' for observation independently of drawing upon his knowledge of it as a resource whereby he constitutes it as a 'topic for investigation'. In this respect his position is no different from that of any other member of society.

TWO: Immersion in a form of life is the necessary and only means whereby an observer is able to generate [knowledge of the world].

D. ONE: Sociological concepts thus obey what I call a double hermeneutic [this means that the subject matter of sociology involves the understanding of other people's understanding].

(A. Giddens, *New Rules of Sociological Method*, Hutchinson, 1976)

Question

1 Discuss the influence of Durkheim, Weber, Schutz, Marx and ethnomethodology in the formulation of these 'rules'.

References and further reading

R. J. Anderson, J. A. Hughes, and W. W. Sharrock, *The Sociology Game*, Longman, 1985.
An introduction to sociological thinking, stressing its pluralistic nature and the problems and difficulties to which this leads.

M. Barrett, *Women's Oppression Today*, Verso, 1980.
A thorough examination of the key issues in feminist thinking about women's oppression, from a feminist–Marxist approach. This is a demanding text but repays careful reading.

R. Bernstein, *The Restructuring of Social and Political Theory*, Methuen, 1976.
Critically covers positivism, interpretivism, phenomenology and the Frankfurt School with the aim of building a new theoretical approach. Not an easy book, but one which is very useful for the detail it provides on particular thinkers.

T. Bottomore, and J. Nisbet (eds), *A History of Sociological Analysis*, Heinemann, 1979.
A collection of 17 essays on virtually every aspect of sociological theory. An extremely useful book which can be dipped into.

I. Craib, *Modern Social Theory*, Harvester, 1984.
A lucid, readable and highly comprehensive introduction to a range of modern theory from Parsons to Habermas. Craib has a rather irreverent and witty approach.

E. C. Cuff and G. C. F. Payne, *Perspectives in Sociology*, George Allen & Unwin, 1984.
Theory is presented as a sequence of different perspectives. The discussion is helpfully backed up by empirical examples.

H. Eisenstein, *Contemporary Feminist Thought*, George Allen & Unwin, 1984.
Focuses on American feminists. Largely concerned with radical feminism. Highly readable.

A. Giddens, *Capitalism and Modern Social Theory*, Cambridge University Press, 1971.
Still the best analysis of Marx, Weber and Durkheim.

————, *Sociology: a Brief but Critical Introduction*, Macmillan, 1986.
A relatively easy introduction to some of the current debates in sociological theory.

————, *Social Theory and Modern Sociology*, Polity Press, 1987.
Addresses a range of issues concerning current developments in sociological theory, relating them to the prospects for sociology in the closing years of the twentieth century.

D. Held, *Introduction to Critical Theory*, Hutchinson, 1980.
A detailed and highly comprehensive overview of the central Frankfurt School thinkers, including Habermas. A demanding but fascinating account of their integration of Marxism and psychoanalysis, and their analyses of capitalism and culture.

P. Rock, *The Making of Symbolic Interactionism*, Macmillan, 1979.
Argues that symbolic interactionism is a major but neglected perspective, although it is responsible for much of the best of modern sociology. Considers its origins and historical development as well as the work of well-known writers such as Becker and Goffman.

R. A. Sydie, *Natural Women, Cultured Men*, Open University Press, 1987.
Examines the work of classical theorists, such as Durkheim, Weber, Engels and Freud, from a feminist perspective.

Index